2.12 - BFT-8/66

ADLAI E. STEVENSON
1900-1965

ADLAI E. STEVENSON
A SHORT BIOGRAPHY

The Conscience of the Country

Adlai E. Stevenson

by STUART GERRY BROWN

BARRON'S WOODBURY PRESS
WOODBURY, NEW YORK

15963

CONTENTS

PREFACE   vii
1. Youth   1
2. Education of a Statesman   23
3. World War II. A Public Career Begins   37
4. Governor of Illinois   54
5. The Campaign of 1952   74
6. Leader of the Opposition, 1953-1956   106
7. From Presidential Candidate to Elder Statesman:
      1956-1960   141
8. Diplomat on the World Stage   174
    APPENDIX   201
    A NOTE ON THE SOURCES   216

Since this volume appears so soon after Governor Stevenson's death, a word of explanation may be in order. The book was commissioned in 1962 as one of a projected series on twentieth century statesmen. Most of the writing was done in 1963; it was revised in the intervals of other work, and finished in the spring of 1965. It went to press a few days before Stevenson's death, so that revisions of tense and a few additions were made in galley proofs.

Thus the book was not hastily prepared. Nor is it in any sense an "official" biography—and it is not intended to be definitive. Its purpose was, and is, to make generally available a usable and readable biography of a great American statesman until such time as another scholar, viewing the man and his time in full perspective, can produce a standard book. When Mr. Barron asked me to undertake this assignment, I was more than a little hesitant, since I had already written one book about Stevenson (*Conscience in Politics*, 1961) and had directed a project of intensive research into the circumstances of the 1960 Democratic nomination and the "Draft Stevenson" movement. (The results of that research will not, for the most part, be available during the lifetimes of many leading figures in the United States government, but they will be useful to Stevenson's eventual biographer.) My reluctance was overcome by the persuasive insistence of several of Stevenson's closest friends and associates—Mrs. Marshall Field, Thomas K. Finletter, John J. B. Shea, Harold Taylor, Mrs. Marietta Tree, and W. Willard Wirtz. I am indebted to all of these people for invaluable information and assistance. None of them, needless to say, is in any way responsible for what I have written.

Governor Stevenson himself was, of course, my chief

source of information. He never could persuade himself that anybody would wish to write about him, but he was generous to a fault with his time and wisdom for anyone who did write about him. It is hard to realize that he has gone. His passing makes me doubly conscious of the shortcomings of this book, but also doubly hopeful that his friends, both near and distant, will find it useful until something better can be done.

University of Hawaii   S.G.B.
July 31, 1965

Youth

I

ON JULY 21, 1952 the International Amphitheatre in the Chicago stockyards was filled to overflowing with delegates to the Democratic National Convention, their friends and families, and with several thousand spectators, all gathered to participate in the opening of a convention which would choose new leadership for the Democratic Party. President Harry S. Truman had decided to retire after the completion of his term in January, 1953. Under Franklin D. Roosevelt and Truman the Democrats had held the White House for twenty years and controlled the Congress for eighteen. Now an old order was changing. The nominee of this convention, whether or not he won the presidency, would replace Truman as leader of the Democratic Party. A new era was about to begin. One of the first speakers the convention would hear was the Governor of Illinois who was scheduled to welcome the delegates. At other conventions in other years other governors had welcomed delegates who were not even there to hear the welcome. Before the speaker would stretch rows of empty seats. Welcoming speeches by mayors and governors are ritual performances at national political conventions.

But this was a different sort of occasion. For most of the delegates were about to see for the first time the elusive and mysterious Governor who would not seek the nomination for President but seemed about to get it anyway—Adlai E. Stevenson. A great burst of applause, growing into a full scale "demonstration," greeted Stevenson's appearance on the rostrum. As he tried to make himself heard over the din his first words were, "I thought I came here to greet you—not you to greet me!" This sally only brought more noise and stirred more enthusiasm among Stevenson partisans on the convention floor. But after a bit the delegates and galleries quieted and sat back to hear what the speaker had to say.

What he said shocked some, delighted others, and perplexed a few of the veteran political observers. One thing was certain; this was not like any other welcoming address. Instead of seizing the opportunity to celebrate the products and beauties of the host state, Stevenson immediately moved from the central point of vantage of the city of Chicago to a major theme:

> Here on the prairies of Illinois and the Middle West, we can see a long way in all directions. We look to east, to west, to north and south. Our commerce, our ideas, come and go in all directions. Here there are no barriers, no defenses, to ideas and aspirations. We want none; we want no shackles on the mind or the spirit, no rigid patterns of thought, no iron conformity. We want only the faith and conviction that triumph in free and fair contest.

The 1952 nominating conventions took place in the unhappy era of American history when Republican Senator Joseph R. McCarthy of Wisconsin was leading a campaign of fear, hate, and slander in the name of opposing Communism. The Governor of Illinois chose as the first order of business to announce his stand for unfettered freedom of thought.

It was an era in which a Democratic Administration was pock-marked with corruption. Cheating, bribery, and influence-peddling in government had been revealed on a shocking scale. The Governor of Illinois had this to say as he welcomed the delegates:

> *Where we have erred, let there be no denial; where we have wronged the public trust, let there be no excuses. Self-criticism is the secret weapon of democracy, and candor and confession are good for the political soul.*

It was an era when Democratic orators, their intellectual capital mostly spent, were often content simply to recall the glories of achievement under Franklin Roosevelt. The Governor of Illinois told the convention:

> *But a great record of past achievement is not enough. There can be no complacency, perhaps for years to come. We dare not just look back to great yesterdays. We must look forward to great tomorrows.*

And conventions are characteristically dominated by personalities—the personality of the presidential nominee above all. The Governor of Illinois struck a different note:

> *What counts now is not just what we are against, but what we are for. Who leads us is less important than what leads us—what convictions, what courage, what faith—win or lose. A man doesn't save a century, or a civilization, but a militant party wedded to a principle can.*

Finally, the Governor of Illinois did not hesitate to lecture the delegates on their manners! "All the world is watching and listening to what we say, what we do and how we behave. So let us give them a demonstration of democracy in action at its best—our manners good, our proceedings orderly and dignified." Flouting tradition and ignoring masses of bunting and banners and the bands poised to blare out their calls to fervor, the Governor of Illinois counselled:

> And—above all—let us make our decisions openly, fairly, not by the processes of synthetic excitement or mass hysteria, but, as these solemn times demand, by earnest thought and prayerful deliberation.

As he 'made this remarkable address, Adlai Stevenson was only just coming into national prominence, and people everywhere were trying to take his measure. In the speech itself—as in the ten years he had already given to public service and in the remainder of a lifetime thereafter to be at the disposal of his countrymen—was underlined an attitude toward politics and public office which has had its advocates since the founding of the republic, yet is often obscured by the more familiar characteristics of the politician as office-seeker. Stevenson, like such founding fathers as Washington, Jefferson, and Madison, stood for the notion that public service is a debt owed by privileged citizens to their country. If a man is able, his ability should be available to his fellow citizens. If they wish him to serve, he should serve. But to seek an office for service must not be confused with seeking an office for power. And the higher the office the more a man should rely upon the judgment of the citizens rather than his own. The American Presidency, Stevenson believed, should seek the man to hold it, not the man the office. It may be that Stevenson's humility in the face of high office ultimately cost him that office, but it endeared him to countless Americans and won him respect everywhere such as few men ever achieve.

After the welcoming address to the delegates at Chicago in 1952, the Stevensonian spirit in American political life was established. And with that spirit of humility and devotion went a remarkable reliance upon reason, upon the quiet, thoughtful handling of great issues. In the years after 1952 Adlai Stevenson became the conscience of American politics. After 1960 he became at times, as he spoke in the United Nations, the conscience of the world. But this was for the future in those July days of 1952. To understand that future well, we must first know the past out of which it came.

II

MUCH HAS BEEN MADE of Adlai Stevenson's distinguished ancestry. The point is not to make too much of it. There is no doubt that Stevenson was always conscious of his inheritance of an obligation to live up to the traditions of gentility and service which marked both sides of his family. But as we examine his background and see him growing up among people of means and social distinction, we must not fall victim of a simple environmentalism. Countless men have emerged from fortunate surroundings without ever achieving distinction in their own right. Few Americans in any generation and with any. background have so well exemplified the virtues they inherited—integrity, idealism, reasonableness, good temper, balanced judgment, magnanimity. The character and achievement of Adlai Stevenson came not from environment alone, nor individual effort alone, but from a healthy interaction between the two.

Adlai Ewing Stevenson II was born in Los Angeles, California on February 5, 1900. In the 1950's when he was running for President his supporters would say that he would be, if elected, "the first President born in this century." There may be a quibble as to whether 1900 or 1901 should be accepted as the first year of the 20th century, but the point itself was not in any case a very good one. To contrast the early life of Stevenson with that of John Fitzgerald Kennedy, for example, is instructive. By the time Kennedy, born in 1917, was 14 years old the post-war boom of the 1920's had collapsed into the worst economic depression ever known in the western world; dictators or would-be dictators like Mussolini, Hitler, and Stalin were front page names; and the world was torn apart by conflicting totalitarianisms. Kennedy was to grow to manhood and live the maturity of his life in a climate of strife and tension—"the bloodiest, most turbulent era of the Christian age," as Stevenson put it in 1952. But when Adlai Stevenson reached the age of 14 on February 5, 1914, the world was still resting, somewhat uneasily to be sure, in the hundred years of peace established by the Concert of Europe at the Congress of Vienna. The United States, since the Civil War, had tended to its own ever more successful business, with time out only for what Theodore Roosevelt called the "spendid little war" in Cuba. The first fourteen years of Stevenson's life, in California and Illinois, were quiet, leisurely years in which tumult and violence seemed far removed from most Americans. Almost at the moment when Archduke Ferdinand was being assassinated, an event which perhaps introduced the characteristic themes of the contemporary world, Stevenson's sister noted in her diary, "Adlai made his first speech today—for the Boys' Anti-Cigarette League." If Adlai Stevenson lived his whole life in the 20th century, it is nevertheless revealing to notice that the seventeen years difference between his birth year and John Kennedy's is the difference between having been born in "the good old days" and in the modern era.

When Adlai Stevenson was born, his father, Lewis Green Stevenson, was a young executive on the Hearst newspapers in California. Between 1900 and 1906 the elder Stevenson's time was divided between Los Angeles and San Francisco, and the family lived for a time in Berkeley. It was good campaign politics, in the 1950's, to remember the birthplace in California and the childhood spent there, but the Stevensons were nevertheless an Illinois family. When Adlai was six his family returned to their home in Bloomington. It was there that he put down his roots and there that he grew to manhood.

And it was in Bloomington that the second Adlai Stevenson came to know the first. Grandfather Adlai E. Stevenson lived in retirement in Bloomington after a long and honored career in public service which had culminated in a term as Vice President of the United States under Cleveland from 1893 to 1897. At his home, only a few doors away, young Adlai found himself on Sundays seated at an old-fashioned family dinner table presided over at one end by his illustrious grandfather and at the other by the sweet and proper old lady who had always called her husband "Mr. Stevenson." It was there, too, that the boy first met the great men of the Democratic Party, like William Jennings Bryan, for the elder Stevensons' home was a natural stopping place for politicians and statesmen traveling through central Illinois.

Adlai attended his first political rally at the age of nine. As he was to do countless times in after years, he sat on the speakers' platform well in the public view. The speakers were his grandfather and Bryan. We do not know how he reacted to the speech of the former Vice President, but his sister, glancing toward him when the storm of applause greeted the conclusion of Byran's oration, observed that her young brother "had gone peacefully to sleep." It may have been this experience which in after years led the future statesman to feel keen sympathy for the somnolence of audiences at political speeches, including his own.

Adlai and his sister, Elizabeth, always known by her nickname "Buffie," went to public schools in Bloomington until their later teens. They lived "on the right side of the tracks," but their friends were chosen for companionship wherever their homes might be. Their father was a natural politician, as their grandfather had been, and perhaps their early experience of outgoing friendliness made it easier for them to mix easily than for some children. Lewis Stevenson was a humorist who shared jokes, anecdotes, and stories of all kinds with his family. His wife, Helen Davis Stevenson, was of Quaker background but by no means lacking in humor.

The household atmosphere was one of gaiety mingled with idealism and the ethics of liberal Protestantism. The family church was Unitarian, but the spiritual influence of Mrs. Stevenson was compounded of many elements, going back to the New England of her ancestors. Her letters to her children, over the years, seldom failed to point a moral to adorn her tale. Adlai Stevenson's characteristic humor is not more suggestive of his father than his moral approach to public affairs is reminiscent of his mother.

On Helen Stevenson's side of the family, the Davises, there was another eminent political ancestor. Helen Stevenson's grandfather was Jesse Fell, one of Lincoln's close friends and co-workers in pre-Civil War Illinois and one of the founders of the Republican Party. Adlai Stevenson was always sensitive to this tenuous line connecting himself with Lincoln. It would be too much to say that the bipartisanship of his family tempered Stevenson's partisanship, but his admiration for Lincoln and his respect for the principles of Lincoln's party in its early years tempered his whole conception of the political party system in the United States. It was not merely political advantage but pride in responsible party processes that led him so often to speak of both his Stevenson and his Fell ancestors in nearly the same breath.

One of the monuments to Jesse Fell's enterprise is the Bloomington newspaper, the *Pantagraph*. When Adlai Stevenson was a boy the paper was owned and managed by his grandfather Davis. But its columns appear to have been open also to the Stevenson side of the family. At any rate Adlai's first article was published in it when he was nine. If this boyish effort gives no forecast of future statesmanship, it does suggest the Stevenson humor and whimsy:

My Pet Bunny

When I was eight years old, my father brought me from his farm a wee bunny that seemed to me no more than three weeks old.

At first bunny was very much frightened. I got a large box for his home and fixed it up very comfortably, where bunny lived cosily for some time, never running away.

His box was kept in the upper half during the night, and one morning when I went out to see how bunny was, I found he was gone. Then everyone in the house started to look for bunny, but nowhere was he to be found until the cook, coming into the dining room saw bunny sitting on a register as comfy as could be. This was only a taste of adventure for bunny, and every day he was in some new mischief. One bright day bunny was sunning himself on a window sill, when a thievish cat suddenly snatched him away. I hunted everywhere, but I could not find him, and I never saw my pet bunny again.

Adlai E. Stevenson
Age 9 years old.

1316 East Washington Street

In later years the *Pantagraph* was to play a central role in Adlai Stevenson's fortunes.

When he was eleven, young Adlai was taken to Europe for a year. This was the first of many voyages and perhaps not the most important for the development of his mind. But his enthusiasms were such as to identify him with American boys of any generation—armor, dungeons, and castles. On one occasion he complained, as petulantly as his easy going, sunny disposition would permit, that he was being required to leave Windsor Castle when "we haven't seen *all* the armor here yet."

The Stevenson family spent some time in England and then made a grand tour of the continent. The winter and spring months were spent at Lausanne, where Adlai was placed in a country day school. Here he quickly learned the French which was to serve him well in years to come, as traveler, statesman, and diplomat.

It was upon his return to the United States in July, 1912

that young Stevenson first became aware of an American statesman who was always to hold a high place in his esteem. Because he thought it was "too hot" in Bloomington, Lewis Stevenson took his family to Spring Lake, New Jersey for a few days. His real purpose seems to have been to be near Governor Woodrow Wilson, the Democratic candidate for President. At any rate, one August afternoon Adlai was taken by his father to call on Wilson. He sat quietly on the porch for several hours while his father and Wilson discussed the campaign. There is no record to show whether his reaction to the future President was as irresistibly sleepy as it had been to William Jennings Bryan, but it is certain that Adlai Stevenson, the statesman of after years, had far more in common with the scholar-politician from New Jersey than with the "Great Commoner" from Nebraska.

Back in Bloomington, during the next winter, there occurred the kind of sudden, unbelievable tragedy that always seems to happen to someone else. The Stevensons were giving a party for the teenage friends of Buffie. Her account of what happened is brief, poignant and accurate:

> One of the boys, home from a military academy, wanted to show us the manual of arms, so we asked Adlai, who was considered too young for the party, to get us a gun. He rushed excitedly to the attic and got Father's .22. After much parading up and down the drawing room, and the usual showing off by boys of that age, the gun was finally returned to my brother to put away. As he went into the hall he must have pulled the trigger a last time, and a bullet that had been stuck in the mechanism was dislodged. The gun went off, the bullet struck my friend Ruth Merwin in the forehead, and she died instantly.

The girl's mother, herself a distant cousin of the Stevensons, was a remarkably sensitive and humane person. Her first thoughts were for the boy who was overcome with grief for what he had inadvertently done. Her encouragement, as well as his own mother's, helped Adlai over the shock and fright until his recuperative powers could bring him back to emotional stability. Neither the Merwins nor the Stevensons ever mentioned the accident again. It was not until reporters asked him about it directly in 1952 that Stevenson himself ever discussed it. He then recalled the episode quietly and factually. That it was a traumatic experience goes without saying. The extent of its effect upon his mind and spirit would be difficult to assess. But many years later an old friend of the Lewis Stevensons told Buffie, now Mrs. Ernest Ives, "your mother knew that tragedy and suffering can wreck a sensitive child for life, or it can deepen and strengthen him. She prayed—and anybody who knows Adlai knows that her prayers were answered."

Stevenson's boyhood was otherwise happy and remarkably healthy. At thirteen he engaged in a running battle with his parents on the question of his being allowed to play football. He was now at the University High School in nearby Normal where the college was another of the monuments to ancestor Jesse Fell. Adlai was strong and stocky. He was not tall but his muscles were well-suited to sports. He had already taken up tennis, enjoyed swimming, and all winter sports. But football, then as now, was somehow thought to be an especially masculine sport. He was asked to go out for the junior team and eagerly sought his parents' permission. He wrote to his mother, who was away from Bloomington at the time:

> *Please telegraph Father to let me play football as you said you would. I have been deprived of that pleasure for so long you ought to let me play this year, as I have been asked to.*
> *. . . I have to write a theme for this afternoon on*

one of the following subjects, an hour in the assembly room an old bridge at sunset or an old fasianed school house. As I know nothing about these it will be pretty hard . . .

with lots of love,
Adlai

P.S. Please don't forget about the football. Please.

If the theme young Stevenson produced that afternoon was no better mechanically than his letter to his mother it was a particularly bad day for him, since he lost the football battle. The following letter suggests how he fared in the debate, and still communicates the characteristic disappointment of a frustrated boy:

Dear Mother: Buffie got your letter this morning in which you said you would not let me play football for another year, that is what you and Father have been telling me for so long, and anyway you promised me you would let me play this fall. If I wait another year I will not be able to play. All doctors say its a bad game but all doctors haven't played it, and more than that they did not play like we play at Normal. Everybody these days have such terrible conceptions of football when they know nothing about it, just because they have read of accidents in for instance a Harvard and Yale game—this is the third Normal team . . . Lots of love,

Adlai

P.S. All the games you mencioned in your letter are out of season.

Athletics in general was a matter of some tension between the boy and his parents for several years. Not the least of the difficulties was lack of a clear signal from father to son. If one can understand the father's problem of resolving his pride in his son's athletic achievements with concern for his health, one cannot help having sympathy also for the vigorous younger Stevenson working hard to hold his own, or better, among other boys at summer camp. When he was fifteen he wrote to his father with some pride about playing third base on the "intermidate" baseball team and being chosen to play singles in an inter-camp tennis match. Father was pleased. "I am so glad," he wrote, "that you are going out for athletics, and that you take the licking you got in such a manly way." On the other hand Lewis Stevenson was concerned about swimming, especially diving. "I wish you would tell me you will stay out of diving contests hereafter. Playing ball is all right, and if I were you I would confine my efforts largely to that." But apparently Adlai was reluctant to accept such restrictions. Before long his father is writing in stern tone, "I must urge you not to go in so much for athletics. I want you to stop this right away." The boy was to have his tonsils out after camp was over and his father was anxious that he should not be "worn out" upon his return home. "I want you to accept my statement, for I mean it, and do exactly as I say." But Adlai was far away from parental supervision. A rigorous hike to the White Mountains was too tempting. Upon his return to camp he wrote his mother that his parents' order not to go arrived only after he had left! With characteristic honesty he added, "I am certainly glad I went now." The tonsils were in due course successfully removed. And though Adlai never achieved athletic prowess, he did become a good club tennis player and built, through walking, hiking, riding, hunting, swimming, and even golf an enviable physical constitution. His aides in the presidential campaigns of later years never could match his pace at walking without discomfort, and his stamina through the gruelling months amazed everyone close enough to him to see what demands campaigning made upon his physical reserves. In 1956, especially, the pace was inhuman. The unexpected necessity of competing for the nomination in a six months primary campaign meant that he was on the campaign roads and lanes and airways for almost a year with hardly more than a few days' rest at any point. Yet he never missed a day or cancelled a commitment because of illness or exhaustion.

The almost idyllic Bloomington boyhood, with its summers at Charlevoix, Michigan or at camp, came to an end when, at sixteen, Adlai Stevenson graduated from University High. He was no scholar, but his poise and winning manner accounted for his being invited to speak at the graduation banquet. Unfortunately and uncharacteristically, no text of his remarks survives. But his sister, who was a guest, long afterward remembered her pride in his poise and that the title of his speech was "To the Senior Celebrities."

III

BEFORE HE WENT AWAY to boarding school Adlai Stevenson was reintroduced to politics. Lewis Stevenson had been appointed Secretary of State of Illinois to fill a vacancy; now, in 1916, he was a candidate for a full term in the state election. It was also a presidential year, and Lewis began his son's summer session in politics by taking him to see the national conventions in Chicago. There he was present at the Bull Moose Convention when Theodore Roosevelt's telegram declining to run was read to the dispirited delegates who forthwith dissolved the Progressive Party. At the Republican convention young Stevenson witnessed the nomination of Charles Evans Hughes. But much to his regret, tutoring for entrance examinations to Choate School in Connecticut prevented his accompanying his father to the Democratic convention in St. Louis, where Woodrow Wilson was nominated for a second term. At home, however, he became an "activist." Working for his father's election, Adlai ran errands, tacked up posters, and distributed literature until the moment of his departure in September. His devotion to his father was now enhanced by a sense of participation in his father's fortunes, so that when news came that Lewis Stevenson had been defeated, Adlai was deeply disappointed. But he took consolation, as did the rest of the family, in the fact that the elder Stevenson ran well ahead of the Democratic ticket in Illinois and President Wilson squeaked to victory. Thirty-two years later Adlai Stevenson more than redeemed the family's political reputation in Illinois by beating his Republican opponent for governor by the largest margin in the history of the state.

Though he was never much better than an average student, young Stevenson passed his entrance exams for Choate and maintained himself in good standing there for two years. In extracurricular activities his star shone more brightly. He made the tennis team, the editorial board of the school paper, and the athletic council. He took a leading part in religious activities. "You didn't know your son was a young evangelist, did you?" he asked his parents when he wrote to announce that he had been elected president of the students' religious club.

It had been planned that Adlai would spend three years at Choate in order to be fully prepared for college. This was to be Princeton, where his Green forbears had gone.* But like other American boys in those days he anxiously watched the war in Europe engulf the world. In the spring of 1918, with no noticeable twinge of regret that he would have to give up the editorship of the *Choate News* as well as other honors for the coming year, Adlai Stevenson enlisted in the Navy as an ordinary seaman.

Instead of the usual summer at a western ranch or at Charlevoix, young Stevenson was assigned to naval barracks at Princeton, where he was a candidate for the student training program. Studying and drilling were now his chief activities. By his own account it was not brilliance but sweat which finally brought him through his academic examinations and gained him admission to the program. Thus his freshman year at college was spent in uniform. Family pride was thereby doubled, since the elder Stevenson had gone into the

---

* Lewis Stevenson's mother was Letitia Green.

Navy also, in a civilian capacity. But Adlai took no pride, then or later, in his "career" in World War I. As a politician, he could joke about it effectively, and he could wear an American Legion cap if occasion required. But he would not hesitate to lecture that same legion on its abuses of patriotism. Stevenson never displayed any flair for things military, and his great service to the Navy, which won him a medal in World War II, was as a civilian official.

With the Great War over and his uniform discarded, Adlai Stevenson settled down to three more happy and satisfying years as a Princeton undergraduate. His genius for friendship was now fully developed and the records of his college life show him almost constantly in company with young men and women. If his grades tended to be "gentleman's C," his social life and his campus activities were straight "A."

His first love, newspaper work, drew his greatest energy. He not only made the board of the *Daily Princetonian* but was elected Managing Editor and saved enough money from his salary in that post to be searching for a good investment after graduation. One of the opportunities suggested to him was to buy into a new magazine publishing enterprise then being launched by two Yale friends, Briten Hadden and Henry Luce. Instead Stevenson chose to back a neighbor in Bloomington who was patenting improvements on a carburetor. Nothing was ever heard again of the carburetor, or of Adlai Stevenson's money. But he must have had moments of genuine regret, especially during his days of political leadership of the Democratic Party, that a decision he made at twenty-three precluded his becoming an owner of *Time* and *Life*.

One of the crowning experiences of Adlai Stevenson's youth came in the summer of his sophomore year when he toured Europe, this time not with family but with Princeton friends. At twenty he was beginning to show signs of becoming something rather more than an average student and "regular fellow" who could be expected, like many of his classmates, to parlay a fortunate inheritance into a successful if stereotyped career in law or business. The boy who, a few years earlier, had wrestled with spelling and feared so painfully his lack of something to say, was evolving into a man who, after a night in the Swiss Alps, could write this:

> I shall never forget that night. It was intensely cold, the moon, full and brilliant and not a cloud in the sky . . . My window faced the Matterhorn which rose like a jagged column of granite out of a sea of sparkling white. Down below me, glittering in the moonlight, lay a vast glacier which occasionally uttered a reverberating groan as the ice cracked or moved slightly.

> In every direction great jagged peaks shot up and stood black against the unearthly blue of the sky, and over all was a choking, maddening silence. The intense cold and clearness of the atmosphere made the stars unbelievably brilliant and everything seemed magnified and brought closer while the real vastness of the scene was inconceivable. It was a sight that I shall never forget and I hardly know whether to call it beautiful or horrible for there was something about it that was awe inspiring and at the same time frightening and supernatural. I could not determine whether to thank God or Satan and in fact I feel sure that there was more of the latter in it . . .

The imagination that was stirred, like Byron's, by the Matterhorn on a clear and moonlit night was stirred in a different and perhaps more profound way by the sight of the battlefields of the Great War. Stevenson and his friends managed to obtain passes to make a tour of the main battlefields along the Western front, where devastation and desolation were often marked by little more than an occasional forlorn tree, or by thousands upon thousands of crosses. It was still too soon to know for sure that the war "to make the world safe for democracy" had in fact made nothing safe. But Stevenson had been aware of Wilson's apparent failure up to that time, and well understood that the fall election would have incalculable consequences. Now, looking from his train window out across the fields where the bloodiest battles in all history had been fought, he tried to imagine their meaning in the long sweep of western civilization. In the next compartment a brilliant girl violinist began to play. The music gave the scene another dimension of emotion and evoked even more somber meditations. It was July 29, the anniversary of the Great War's beginning. Later that summer, Stevenson and his friends toured the battlefields of Belgium. These, wrote Adlai to his parents, were "practically paved with iron, and although it had been cleaned up, I found lots of unexploded shells, hand grenades, etc." These images—desolation, music, cemeteries, and remnants of arms —were to stay with him all his life. Though Stevenson never became a pacifist, there is no doubt that his ceaseless efforts, in the 1950's and 1960's, to show the world the way to peace had their remote origins in those long ago experiences.

Upon his return from Europe in September, 1920, Stevenson became as active as he could in the presidential election. Though he was not yet old enough to vote, he could speak and electioneer whenever opportunity presented itself. He helped establish the Cox-Roosevelt Club at Princeton in the conviction that Governor James Cox of Ohio and Assistant Secretary of the Navy Franklin D. Roosevelt of New York were far more likely to secure the stability and freedom of the world in the wake of the war than were Senator Warren Harding of Ohio and Governor Calvin Coolidge of Massachusetts. But in young Stevenson's mind the candidates were less important than were the ideas of President Wilson which, rightly as it turned out, seemed to him the real issue of the election. More than thirty years later, addressing another generation of Princetonians, Adlai Stevenson recalled

the mood of that earlier day when the Wilsonian dream
was not yet wholly dissolved:

> A terrible war to make the world safe for democracy had
> just ended victoriously. A noble concept, the League of
> Nations, had emerged from the chaotic aftermath of that
> elemental struggle. It was the twilight of kings, the dawn
> of world-wide democracy. Optimism was boundless and
> people proclaimed that we were on the threshold of the
> new era of universal and perpetual peace and prosperity.
> It didn't turn out that way . . .

In retrospect Stevenson did himself less than justice by re-
membering only the optimism. His enthusiasm in 1920 was
in fact moderated by his fears that the people were not yet
ready for Wilson's covenant. When Cox and Roosevelt
were defeated he was saddened, but not taken by surprise.
But he was young and the setback seemed temporary. Soon
he was again engrossed in more personal tasks and pleasures.

In the 1950's, when Adlai Stevenson was the object of
national interest almost daily and when, in the literary world,
there was a vigorous revival of F. Scott Fitzgerald, the two
men were frequently linked in discussions of Stevenson's
youth. Stevenson did indeed lead an active and happy social
life in those days. He was a good dancer and a welcome
guest at week-end house parties. He shared the gaiety of the
Twenties both in college life and in summer tours in Europe.
He liked to write and had ambitions to make his living by
his pen. And he loved Princeton with a passion. But the
parallel ends there. Stevenson met Fitzgerald only casually
and never moved in the older man's circle. Nor was he given
to the kind of frenetic search for values and meaning in life
which ended, for Fitzgerald, in tragic futility. Stevenson's
liberal religious outlook, his habit of disciplining himself to
moderation, and his ideals of progress for mankind and the
social obligation of the individual were well-formed. The

cynicism of the "Lost Generation" rubbed against him but did not rub off on him.

Stevenson's Princeton career was successful in most respects. He never became a scholar, but he absorbed much from lectures and books. He made lasting friendships, and won the respect and affection of his entire class. He was elected to Whig Hall, the ancient debating society, to the Senior Council, and even received a few votes as "most likely to succeed." The winner in the latter contest, a life-long friend of Stevenson's, was Everett Case who became President of Colgate University and afterwards President of the Sloan Foundation. Other friends were T. S. Matthews, who was to be one of the most eminent journalists of his time, and John Marshall Harlan, whose distinguished career in the law was crowned by his appointment to the Supreme Court.

But no doubt the most solid satisfaction of Stevenson's Princeton years was his work on the *Daily Princetonian*. He worked hard all four years, first to make the board of the paper, and then to make it a better paper. His election as Managing Editor for his senior year brought him an opportunity to see what he could do in an executive post, and he did well. It also gave him an unwelcome opportunity to display the humility which was always the central mark of his character. Unfortunately, Lewis Stevenson had little humility when his son's achievements were in his mind. He reported Adlai's appointment to the *Princetonian* as though Managing Editor were the top position. Adlai was infuriated. He told his father so in a vigorous letter:

> Dear Father: Once more may I protest (as usual in vain I suppose) against your assumption of the duties of my publicity manager. As in the past, when I have strenuously objected, you have nevertheless gone ahead and with the apparent intent of pleasing a mere child, put things in papers which were altogether wrong in point of

*fact and most embarrassing to me. And now again: as-
sailed from all sides with clippings from the Chicago
Tribune to the effect that I am head of the Princetonian
when as a matter of fact I am only second. Consequently
many stories about how it got in, can't understand it, etc.
Please desist and do me a real favor . . .*

As Stevenson's Princeton years neared their close in the
spring of 1922 he was full of uncertainty as to what course
he would pursue thereafter. His father was strongly in favor
of law school. Hoping, perhaps, that his son would take up
a career in politics or public service, Lewis wished to make
certain that he had the preparation for such a life that he
himself had missed. Lewis had not gone to college and in his
public posts had always felt that a legal education would
have served him well. The law would, in any case, be good
training for business if that should be Adlai's bent. But the
prospect of law school was not pleasing to the son. He wanted
to write, though he was not at all sure what kind of writing
he could do. He wanted, for a time at least, to be a newspaper man. At his father's insistence he gained admission to
the Harvard Law School, and then, right after Commencement, set out again for Europe with several friends, his mind
still not settled. During that summer he spent some time with
his sister in Switzerland. To her he confided that he hoped to
persuade his father to be satisfied if he spent one year in law
school. After that he wanted a year at Oxford and then work
on a London paper. Later, perhaps, he would "join the re-
organizers of the Diplomatic Corps." Did Buffie think Father
would be "very mad?" Apparently Father was, since Adlai,
recognizing his financial dependence, withdrew his suggestion
and settled down in September, 1922 at the Harvard Law
School.

Life in Cambridge, Stevenson found, was greatly different from Princeton. For one thing, he had to study far harder
than he had ever done before, just to keep in good standing.

He informed his parents that at least half the men were flunked out after a year, or even less. But he found that by investing half the hours of the day in his reading and briefs he could manage to stay above the academic water line. Another sharp difference from the accustomed life at Princeton was the absence of extra-curricular activities. There was no paper to work for, nor social clubs to fill up idle time. There were eating clubs where the conversation typically turned on problems of the law, and there was, at the end of a dim road ahead, the *Harvard Law Review*. But though he could hold his own in the conversations, Stevenson had no illusions about being able to make the law review. Social life was confined mainly to week-end house parties and an occasional theatre or concert. But it was a good life and Adlai Stevenson found that he liked it. Among many new friends was Francis Plimpton who became his roommate and, forty years later, joined him as a diplomat at the United Nations.

But in the spring of 1924 his Harvard career ended abruptly. In Bloomington his uncle Bert Davis, editor and publisher of the *Pantagraph*, died, leaving the paper, through an ambiguous will, partly to the Merwins and partly to the Stevensons. Adlai, home for the funeral, found himself inevitably involved in *Pantagraph* problems, and decided to drop out of Harvard. He was just holding his own academically at the time, and after prolonged absence he was persuaded that he would not pass his final examinations if he tried them. It seemed best to withdraw and accept the family's invitation to go to work on the *Pantagraph*. There is no doubt that this decision marked the end of Stevenson's growing-up years. He was the rare sort of man whose education would continue throughout his life, but henceforth that education was to be conducted chiefly in a world of action. Princeton and Harvard receded into the background, leaving a soft illumination of mind and imagination always to be cherished, but never to "tag" the man.

2

Education of a Statesman

BEFORE SETTLING TO WORK in earnest on the *Pantagraph*,
Adlai Stevenson had another chance to observe the drama
of presidential politics close-up. In June, 1924 he was guest
of his father at the Democratic convention at Madison
Square Garden in New York City when John W. Davis was
nominated on the 103d ballot. To be Lewis Stevenson's guest
was an advantage that year since he was both the honorary
secretary of the convention and the campaign manager for a
dark horse candidate for President, David F. Houston who
had been Secretary of Agriculture in Wilson's cabinet. Adlai
Stevenson had many opportunities to look behind the scenes.
At the Houston headquarters in the Hotel Saville he heard
much interesting gossip and saw some of the attempts made
by the Houston managers to pry loose delegates pledged to
Alfred E. Smith or William G. McAdoo, as the deadlock of

the convention seemed more and more unlikely to be resolved in favor of either of the leaders. At the Smith and McAdoo headquarters he saw the feverish and bone-tiring activity that men go through when they have a chance for the great prize. But whether he simply absorbed the sophisticated wisdom of some of his elders or quickly developed a political perspicacity of his own, he wrote to his mother very early in the convention that "it looks more and more as if John W. Davis was the man." Davis it was, apparently without eliciting much enthusiasm from either of the Stevensons. At any rate Adlai was not active in the campaign, preferring to devote his time and energies to learning his new job on the *Pantagraph*.

That valuable paper was the object of a friendly lawsuit instituted by the Merwins and the Stevensons to determine the ownership. Pending the outcome it was agreed that both Davis Merwin and Adlai Stevenson would work on the paper as representatives of their families. For Adlai this was an opportunity he had not dared to hope for. He grasped it with characteristic enthusiasm and diligence. Nominally he was an editor, but he gave much of his time to reporting. His sister recalled in later years that Lloyd Lewis, one of the leading professional writers of the period, had called Stevenson "the best natural born reporter" he had ever known. Mrs. Ives cited an example which suggests that Lewis's estimate was not merely the sentimental rhetoric of a friend. In the summer of 1924 Stevenson covered the story of a tornado that had caused great devastation around Murphysboro, Illinois. Here, in part, is his story in the *Pantagraph*:

> I saw a farmer dressed in his best blue suit, pale but dry-eyed and composed, push his way through a crowd in front of a morgue and emerge a moment later carrying a tiny white casket not three feet long. He placed the casket tenderly beside him in his Ford and drove away. That was Mary, aged two. Baby Jane is still inside; he will come back for her.

> . . . A little girl sits quietly weeping on a pile of rub-
> bish, hugging a shattered doll. A cow wanders aimlessly
> and hungrily among the smoking ruins. An old lady was
> sitting with her aged husband. She was unharmed; of
> him, there remained to her two limbs and a watch with
> the crystal intact . . . The few available hearses in Mur-
> physboro are racing back and forth to the cemetery, car-
> rying two caskets at a time. Of formal funerals there are
> none, but of heroic fortitude there is much.

Writing like this shows well enough that Stevenson's leaning
toward newspaper work, or at the least toward writing of some
sort, was a leaning in the right direction.

As an editor Stevenson's best work was done in 1925 in
a series of editorials on the Scopes trial in Dayton, Tennessee. There the high school teacher, John Scopes, was being
tried for violation of the Tennessee law forbidding the teach-
ing of biological evolution in the public schools. William
Jennings Bryan was advisory counsel and witness for the state,
while Clarence Darrow headed a distinguished panel of defense lawyers. Stevenson found himself immediately in sympathy with Scopes. Unhappily this conviction placed him
against Bryan, the friend of his grandfather and the idol of his
own boyhood. But he saw, and asserted, the shoddy quality of
Bryan's argument. His editorials deplored the Tennessee statute and the bigotry and censorship it fostered in the schools
of the state. His language had not yet the depth he was to
command in later years, but the conviction and the spiritual
courage to utter it point from these youthful editorials to a
statement like this almost thirty years later:

> It is said that religious creeds are written to mark the
> graves where heresies lie buried. There is a common her-
> esy and its graves are to be found all over the earth. It is
> the heresy that says you can kill an idea by killing a man,
> defeat a principle by defeating a person, bury truth by
> burying its vehicle. Man may burn his brother at the
> stake, but he cannot reduce truth to ashes; he may mur-

der his fellow man with a shot in the back, but he does not murder justice; he may even slay armies of men, but as it is written, "truth beareth off the victory."

Thus, in 1952, did Governor Adlai E. Stevenson of Illinois dedicate the memorial to Elijah Lovejoy, martyr to freedom of speech.

The suit over ownership of the *Pantagraph* went all the way to the Illinois Supreme Court, where it was settled in favor of the Stevensons. But their legal victory turned out to be a hollow one, since the Merwins had managed to acquire a small block of stock that had been owned outside the family. This gave them a majority of the voting shares, and cousin Adlai Stevenson's newspaper career was jolted off its tracks for good.

Again he looked toward the law, but again without enthusiasm. Perhaps his views were modified somewhat by a long conversation with Justice Oliver Wendell Holmes in Washington. Stevenson was in Washington to attend the wedding of his friend Charles Denby, then a secretary to Justice Holmes. Through Denby he found an opportunity to meet the great jurist, and ever afterwards cherished both the kindness and the wisdom he found in that memorable afternoon's conversation. It would be too much to say that Stevenson returned to Bloomington with his course set freshly toward the law. But he did accept his father's suggestion that he enroll at Northwestern to finish his law training. During the academic year 1925-1926 he attended classes at Evanston from Monday to Friday and worked on the *Pantagraph* on the week-ends. This time there was no question of his standing and he not only graduated promptly in June, 1926 but shortly thereafter passed the examinations for admission to the Illinois bar. He was ready to go into a law office—but not yet quite willing.

Like many another restless and enterprising young American, Adlai Stevenson had a yearning for a hitch as a foreign correspondent. The months immediately following his admission to the bar seemed likely to offer his last chance. Still on the staff of the *Pantagraph*, he decided to have a try at visiting the Soviet Union as a working journalist. With his father's help he obtained credentials as a correspondent also for International News Service and the Chicago *Herald-American*. And toward the end of July Stevenson sailed for Europe, accompanied on the first leg of his journey by his mother and sister. After a tour of Italy he wrote about fascism and Mussolini for the *Pantagraph* in language such as he might well have used twenty or thirty years later:

> It is evident that to insure its position and the safety of its chief, Fascism has adopted the same tactics that Communism has in Russia, though under considerably different circumstances. Historically, suppression leads to violence. Taking away free speech is taking away the safety valve. Imagine being liable to imprisonment for the mere expression of an antipathetic point of view, no matter how sincere! . . . It is evident that order has come out of chaos, but the "beneficent tyrant" has conferred these benefits by locking the lazy, quarrelsome boy [Italy] in a straight jacket, stuffing a handkerchief in his mouth, and then hypnotizing him with juggling feats performed with sticks of dynamite.

This kind of analysis was the more significant since it was written at a time when many Americans, even including such a beloved comic sage as Will Rogers, were loud in their approval of Mussolini and the "order" he had brought to Italy where, to the delight of American tourists, the trains at last ran on time.

Leaving his traveling companions, Stevenson went on to Budapest where with the help of a friend in the United States Embassy he attempted to obtain a visa for Russia. His objective was to interview the Soviet Foreign Minister, Chicherin, who had up to that time refused to see Western correspondents. Stevenson told his friends that he thought the very fact that he was young and unknown might persuade Chicherin to see him, though the veteran writers were systematically turned down. But for a good while Stevenson could not even get into Russia. In Budapest he was flatly told "no." He moved on to Belgrade where the Russian consul denied his request. At Bucharest he had the same experience. In Sofia he was again turned down. But at Constantinople, the last chance, he was so persistent that the Soviet consul there finally relented and gave him the necessary papers.

Boarding a small Italian freighter on the Black Sea, Stevenson finally arrived at Batum in the Russian Caucasus. There he was searched and most of his papers and books confiscated. But he was then released and allowed to go on his way. He traveled first to Tiflis and then to Baku where he took a train for Moscow. On the way he stopped at Rostov-on-Don, Kharkov, and Kiev, all of which were to be scenes of bitter fighting in World War II. There and in Moscow Stevenson was impressed by the piteous poverty of the people, and by their evident fear of authority. He himself never knew for certain whether he was being watched, but he felt the reluctance of Russians to be seen in his company lest they be questioned by the police.

In Moscow he joined the small American-European colony and went to work on his plan to interview Chicherin. Day after day Stevenson applied at the Foreign Commissariat, and each day was told to come back later. Meanwhile he was guided about the city and introduced to many people by the Countess Tolstoy, then curator of the Tolstoy Museum. Among the people he met was Karl Radek, one-time German revolutionary and later editor of *Pravda* and a close friend of Lenin's. Radek was a victim of the great purge trials of the 1930's, though not executed as Stevenson supposed.

Stevenson's observations in Russia were clear and his reactions articulate. He saw not only the poverty and the brutality of the dictatorship, but felt the inevitable relationship between the misery of the people and the fraudulence of a dictatorship which claimed to represent the masses. His experience removed any temptation he might otherwise have felt to look leftward during the depression years of the 1930's. Unlike many of his contemporaries, Adlai Stevenson never was attracted by utopian visions. His love of his country, not simply because it was his but because of its freedom and its spiritual strength, grew rather than diminished as his experience of the world broadened.

But he failed in the specific object of his mission to Moscow. On more than one occasion, he recalled afterwards, he felt certain that the Russian Foreign Commissar was listening just behind the closed door as the young American argued and pleaded with officials in the outer office. But he was put off so many times that at last he was forced to accept defeat and turn about for home. On the way back he visited Leningrad for several days, and then went on through Finland and Sweden to Western Europe. He reached home in the middle of October, 1926. Shortly thereafter he went to work in Chicago for the law firm of Cutting, Moore, and Sidley.

It was an abrupt transition. For seven years Adlai Stevenson worked hard at the law and took a full and happy part in the social life of Chicago. In 1929 he married pretty, vivacious Ellen Borden, and they built a comfortable home in the country at Libertyville, Illinois. As a young lawyer-commuter his life was full and interesting. But it was not quite wholly in character. Friends of these Chicago days, who were surprised at Adlai Stevenson's emergence into national prominence in the 1940's, had not known the Stevenson of the *Pantagraph* and the tour of Russia. There were some important exceptions, however. Friends like Hermon Smith, the Edison Dicks, the Marshall Fields, and George Ball saw in Stevenson from the beginning a depth of understanding of world affairs, an appreciation of the American system of government, and a desire to serve which flowered slowly. When the moment came in the 1940's these friends were among

Stevenson's foremost supporters and co-workers, even though several were Republicans.

In 1928 Adlai Stevenson again attended the Democratic National Convention, where Alfred E. Smith was nominated. His own father was honored by serious consideration as a possibility for the vice-presidential nomination. The younger Stevenson was proud of his father and enthusiastic for Smith. But he saw no real chance of defeating Herbert Hoover in the fall election. Though he could not have known it, his own analysis of American politics was remarkably like that of Franklin D. Roosevelt. The latter had decided in the early Twenties, during his recovery from infantile paralysis, that the Republicans would hold the White House until a severe economic recession shook the popular confidence in their program of "normalcy." Roosevelt was mistaken only in his guess that Republican hegemony would last until 1936. In 1928, however, prosperity was so high and the prestige of Hoover, the Republican candidate, so great that Governor Smith's cause was probably lost at the outset. Stevenson, of course, supported Smith despite the Republican complexion of his conservative law firm. But his working energies were mainly devoted to his law work, and his reputation as a skilled and indefatigable lawyer slowly grew. The firm encouraged him with raises in salary and the prospect of an eventual partnership.

During these years Stevenson's interest in world affairs continued in a subdued key. He read a great deal and followed world events carefully. In time he joined the Chicago Council on Foreign Relations, then being promoted by an able journalist and correspondent, Clifford Utley. At the Council meetings Stevenson made the acquaintance of many international figures who went there to speak. Sometimes he served as chairman of the meetings. On such occasions his own speaking was so appropriate and effective that he found himself becoming a leader of the organization. In the winter of 1933 he was elected its president. By the end of the decade the platform provided by the Council was to bring Stevenson to national attention. But meanwhile there was to be an interlude of service in Washington as a "New Dealer."

When the Great Depression set in after the stock market crash in the fall of 1929, Stevenson began to feel restive. As he saw unemployment mounting in Chicago, the values of property rapidly declining despite the efforts of law firms like his own to shore them up, and the tide of human misery generally rising, he felt a growing desire to take some more active part in the attempt to bring the nation out of the doldrums.

The election of Franklin D. Roosevelt to the Presidency in 1932 gave Stevenson, like hundreds of other young American professional men, the chance he was searching for. George Peek, old time Progressive agricultural reformer and friend of Lewis Stevenson, became head of the Agricultural Adjustment Administration (AAA) in the spring of 1933 and quickly set out to bring the best younger men he could find to Washington. When Adlai Stevenson was recommended to him, he said, "Why, that is Louie Stevenson's boy—and he ought to be well back-grounded in farm problems, all right. Let's get him if we can."

Stevenson answered the call to Washington promptly, taking a post in July, 1933 as assistant to Jerome Frank, then Counsel to AAA. He found Washington an exciting, vibrant place, filled with the creative confusion of men vigorously seeking solutions to the problems of low prices, unemployment, and declining living standards. The New Dealers were agreed with the President that government had a prime responsibility to set the nation on its feet again. Their disagreements were on questions of how it was to be done. Stevenson found the work not only exciting but congenial. He described his work in a letter to his wife:

> *The work is complicated but interesting and vastly important. In essence we're creating gigantic trusts in all the food industries, to raise prices and eliminate unfair com-*

petition, thereby increasing returns to the farmer ultimately. Everyone from flour millers to mayonnaise man-
ufacturers are here and each day I hear all about the
troubles of a different industry in conferences, then spend
the night drafting a remarketing agreement to correct
them. Then the objections begin to flow in from all over
the country. Finally we hold public hearings, and at last
the Sec'y of Ag. signs and approves the agreement, etc.,
etc. The procedure is complicated—too complicated. I
would like to tell you about it but it would take forever.
Furthermore, it is changed almost daily! If anything, my
complaint would be that there is too much drafting by
the legal division and too little administering—but I
hope the situation will be corrected when we get a better
background of experience.

Adlai Stevenson may not have been as well "back-
grounded" in farm matters as George Peek anticipated. But
he had a sound general understanding of the continuing
problems of low prices and over-production which had plagued
the American farmer since World War I. His father had
been the manager of many thousands of acres of farm land
and Adlai had often, over the years, visited the farms with
him and talked agriculture. But perhaps the more valuable
legacy Lewis, who died in 1929, had left to his son was a
sense of having been initiated into public affairs. Through his
father he had met many of the men who were taking over
the posts of power in Washington in 1933. Some of them
he had known all his life. To serve in the government was of
course a new experience, but he felt spiritually at home.

In 1933 the Prohibition Amendment was repealed and
a federal agency was set up to reestablish the alcohol industry and regulate its activities. The Alcohol Control Administration, as it was known, was a subsidiary agency of the
AAA and recruited some of its staff from the parent body.
Adlai Stevenson was asked to go into its legal division. In
January, 1934, he became Assistant General Counsel of the

Alcohol Control Administration. In this capacity he served until September, writing codes of pricing and distribution regulations for alcoholic beverages. When this work was completed, Stevenson decided it was time to go home. He had had leave of absence from his law firm, but no assurance that his advancement would not suffer from his absence. If he was not to become a government careerist he knew it was time to return to the law. And his need for income was greater now, with a wife and two young sons, Adlai III and Borden. John Fell, the Stevensons' third son was born in 1936.

Stevenson's reputation as an effective younger leader in civic and national affairs grew rapidly in the next few years. He was appointed to various boards under New Deal agencies, continued his work on the Council on Foreign Relations, and was appointed to boards and directorships of such civic organizations as Hull House and the Immigrants Protective League. In 1935 he became a partner in the Cutting, Moore, and Sidley firm. On several occasions he was urged to go again to Washington as a government official. One offer was to be Commissioner of Naturalization and Immigration. Another suggestion, for which Senator J. Hamilton Lewis of Illinois was intermediary, was that he become Assistant Attorney General of the United States. Such positions he declined with regret. To serve the government in such important capacities would have been both interesting and satisfying to his conscientious wish to be of use. But he did not envision himself as a career government official. And as the situation in Europe became more and more menacing he found his attention absorbed rather by international affairs. If he had been offered a diplomatic post in those days, or a post in the State Department, he probably would have accepted. Instead he stayed in Chicago, continuing to work ten hour days at his law practice, but devoting more and more "spare time" to the Council on Foreign Relations.

When World II broke out in September, 1939, Stevenson soon found himself engaged in the great battle of ideas that divided the United States until December 7, 1941. The question was whether the United States should risk involvement in the war by openly siding with the Western allies or seek to maintain a safe isolation from foreign wars and quarrels. In Chicago, the isolationist capitol was Colonel Robert McCormick's *Chicago Tribune*, while the leading internationalist paper was Colonel Frank Knox's *Chicago Daily News*. In the meetings of the Council on Foreign Relations the issue was debated continually and hotly, until it became apparent that a great majority of the members, including Knox, were ranging themselves on the internationalist side. The *Tribune* began to denounce the Council and such leaders as Knox, Utley, and Stevenson as "warmongers." For their part, the internationalists felt and expressed the view that the isolationists were giving assistance, perhaps unintentionally, to Hitler.

In the winter of 1939-1940 some of the Council members, among them Knox and Stevenson, joined in forming a national organization to express sympathy with the Western allies and try to influence public opinion to see that the success of the Allies would be the best defense for the United States. The new organization, known as the Committee to Defend America by Aiding the Allies, was headed by William Allen White, editor of the Emporia, Kansas, *Gazette*, a veteran Republican progressive whom Stevenson had always admired. He was proud to accept when he was asked by White and others to head the Chicago branch of the national committee.

In the spring of 1940 Hitler invaded the Low Countries and Scandinavia, deepening the threat to the West and the peril to the United States. In the new crisis President Roosevelt brought two eminent Republicans, former Secretary of State Henry L. Stimson and Colonel Frank Knox, into his cabinet. Stimson became Secretary of War and Knox took over the Navy Department. Between Knox, who had been Republican candidate for Vice President in 1936, and Stevenson a warm friendship had developed over their years of association in the Council on Foreign Relations. Knox, Stevenson's senior by twenty years, was not troubled that his friend was a Democrat. He admired Stevenson for his obvious integrity, his reliance on reason, and his high principles. When Knox was called to Washington as Secretary of the Navy he almost immediately talked to Stevenson about going with him as an assistant. But the two men agreed that for the time being, at any rate, Stevenson was more urgently needed in Chicago to continue the campaign of support for the Allies.

In that campaign, during the winter of 1940-1941, Stevenson learned how bitter and cruel partisanship in politics and public affairs can be. As the war deepened and the Committee to Defend America by Aiding the Allies pleaded ever more strongly for American aid to Britain and France, the isolationists became abusive. The Chicago *Tribune* began making editorial attacks on Stevenson personally. He was a "warmonger," "a blood-thirsty Anglophile," etc. His Committee, said the McCormick paper and the broadside literature of the America First Committee, was selling the United States down the river in the interests of a foreign power. Stevenson, for his part, found himself moving toward greater and greater commitment to the Allied cause. If Britain went down, he believed, the United Sates would find itself isolated in a hostile world. Britain could not hold on without massive American support. It would be necessary to arm the American convoys of merchant ships to Britain, and Stevenson argued for that policy. He vigorously supported President Roosevelt's trade of destroyers for bases in the West Indies. And, breaking at last with White, the national Committee and Stevenson himself gave full support to President Roosevelt's plan for a "lend-lease" program to give maximum aid to the countries willing to fight Hitler and Mussolini. The *Tribune* now became so abusive that Stevenson felt obliged to answer. In a letter for their readers' column he wrote:

> We think Hitler is a menace and detests democracy; he has said so. We think Britain is engaged in a death struggle to stop that menace. We think that, with our help, she can succeed. . . . We know that no more aid for Britain would be great news in Berlin—and evidently in some quarters in this country.

The *Tribune* headlined this communication "From America Second." Later, in reply to an invitation to debate an America First representative, he wrote, in language strikingly like the characteristic Stevenson of later years:

> I hope and pray that this issue can and will be presented to the people henceforth with the restraint and responsibility it deserves. Sincere, patriotic Americans can honestly disagree. . . . There has been too much suspicion, too many epithets, too little reason. The decisions we make this winter will affect our future for years, perhaps generations. Let us approach them in our best, not our worst, national tradition.

In retrospect one can hear in such words as these the voice of the Governor of Illinois, addressing the Democratic National Convention and the American people in 1952, or the American Delegate of the 1960's speaking in the United Nations on the crises of that later time. Adlai Stevenson was forty-one years old in 1941, and his intellectual, rhetorical, and imaginative powers were rapidly maturing. He was ready for service now on a broader stage. When, in May, Secretary Knox called him and asked him to go to Washington as the Assistant to the Secretary, Stevenson responded with enthusiastic dedication. He could not, of course, have known it, but his career as a statesman was about to begin.

3

World War II. A Public Career Begins

I

WHEN ADLAI STEVENSON RETURNED to work in Washington in May, 1941, after an absence of seven years, the United States had the same President he had served back in New Deal days, and there was something of the same intensity and bustle among government workers. Otherwise it was like a different world. During his first period in Washington Stevenson had had a part in a great creative effort to lift a nation into prosperity. Priority then went to ideas. But in 1941 all energies were bent to the task of shoring up the nation's defenses against what looked like an inevitable clash with the totalitarians. The priority now was upon speed. The front line was Britain, fighting Hitler alone, in Europe, Africa, and on the seas. The United States had at once to build an army, a navy, and an air force of modern caliber and overwhelming strength, and to keep a steady and increasing flow of weapons and

37

planes and ships moving to the British. World War II was throughout characterized by an industrial competition to the death between the United States, with what help she could get from Britain, Canada, and, later, the Soviet Union, and the German-Italian-Japanese Axis powers. Heroism on the battlefield, in the air, or on the oceans could win little more advantage toward the outcome of the war than industrial production and movement of war material would permit.

It was this behind-the-lines industrial war in which Stevenson played his important part. Thus one of his first assignments was to try to forestall a strike at the Kearny shipyards in New Jersey. Representing Secretary Knox in both the formal and informal efforts at mediation he saw all hope of a settlement at last disappear. On August 7, 1941 the strike began. Since a shutdown could not be tolerated, Knox and Stevenson immediately made preparations for the government to take over the yards. The order for the takeover required the signature of the President. But Roosevelt was at that moment at sea somewhere in the North Atlantic, meeting Prime Minister Winston Churchill to draft and publish what became known as *The Atlantic Charter*.

Stevenson was sent off to find the President. He carried with him not only the order to take over the shipyards but a secret message to be delivered to the President personally. The message was that a "usually reliable source" had informed one of the senior admirals that Stalin had that day opened negotiations to make peace with Hitler. The Germans had invaded Russia less than two months previously and were then cutting great gaps in the Russian lines, racing toward Moscow. A separate peace between the Soviet Union and Germany would leave Great Britain not only once more alone, but faced by a Germany secure in the rear and vastly strengthened. It was terrifying news, and Stevenson started on his mission in a mood of deep discouragement. He was flown to Rockland, Maine whence he was to be flown directly to the cruiser *Augusta*. But at Rockland he found that the *Augusta* had already docked and the President had departed in his special train. Despite bad weather Stevenson's pilot then flew him to Portland where he could wait for the arrival of the train. But when he reached the railroad station he found an immense crowd of people waiting to cheer the President. Stevenson even had difficulty in boarding the train, since he was not known to the police or Secret Service men. Finally, however, he was recognized by Senator Claude Pepper and, after further delay, he was allowed to go to the dining car where the President, with Mrs. Roosevelt, Harry Hopkins, and two aides, was finishing dinner.

The President greeted him cordially, by his first name, and listened quietly to his message about the shipyard strike. But, to Stevenson's dismay, Mr. Roosevelt thought the matter could wait until the next day when he would meet with Knox and others in Washington. Many years later Stevenson recalled the conversation which followed:

> " 'But, Mr. President,' I said, 'this executive order should be signed right now!'
>
> " 'I think it will work out all right this way,' said the President.
>
> " 'Well,' I said, 'if you say so I guess it will be O.K.' I marvel that I could have talked like such a fool, but I was so nervous I hardly knew what I was saying—mostly, I suppose, because I hadn't yet said the really important thing—the message—and I didn't know how to deliver it with all those people sitting around. I could see he was waiting for me to leave, and I had to come out with something. The talk went about like this:
>
> " 'I have something else to tell you, Mr. President.'
>
> " 'Do you, Adlai? What is it?'
>
> " 'Well, Mr. President, it's a message from Admiral ———. He said to tell you . . . alone.'
>
> " 'Oh, I think you can tell me here, Adlai.'
>
> " 'No, sir, I can't.' I had a feeling that everyone was doing his best to keep from laughing! I had an idea, just in time. 'Can I write it down, sir?'

" 'Why, certainly.'

"I took the menu and I wrote on the back of it, 'Admiral —— has heard from a heretofore reliable source today that Stalin has started negotiations with Hitler.'

"Then I gave him back the menu. He read it carefully and then looked up at me.

" 'Adlai,' he said, 'do you believe this?'

"That was too much! I didn't know what I thought. 'Why, I don't know, Mr. President,' I stammered.

" 'I don't believe it,' said F.D.R., 'I'm not worried at all. Are you worried, Adlai?'

"I said I guessed I wasn't so much worried after all. Then, mission completed after a fashion, I took my departure, and in my embarrassed confusion, I wheeled around and crashed right into a closed door, thus bending my crooked nose some more."

The next day the President did indeed issue the order to take over the Kearny shipyards, and, of course, Stalin never did deal with Hitler. But Stevenson's serio-comic mission was successful in another way. Despite the incongruity of the scene, he made an excellent impression on President Roosevelt and thereafter had the full confidence of the President.

Stevenson never knew President Roosevelt intimately, but he had frequent meetings with him during the war. As deputy for Secretary Knox he often took part in important conferences on Navy policy, and as Knox's representative on various wartime boards and commissions he had many opportunities to participate with the President in the formulation of national defense policy.

Stevenson's duties never involved specifically military affairs, but he did have responsibilities, on behalf of the Secretary of the Navy, for personnel administration. From the outset he was disturbed to see the way in which the Navy segregated its negro sailors. Stevenson's own conviction had always been that the United States should be the land of equal opportunity, regardless of race, creed, or color. Discrimination among men who were fighting for that land seemed a double insult to the ideals of the nation. He first took the matter up with Secretary Knox, who expressed agreement and suggested that Stevenson see what could be done to end the segregation policy. Stevenson, for his part, talked privately and quietly with both civilian and military naval officials, arguing simply that to discriminate on the basis of color was no better than to discriminate on the basis of race as Hitler did. Since segregation was traditional in the Navy, Stevenson found a good deal of resistance to any plans to break it down. Finally, with Knox's approval, he went to the President to present his position. The Commander-in-Chief was delighted that such an initiative was coming from the Navy itself, even if the leadership of the Navy was less than unanimous. He gave Stevenson the backing he needed, and the segregation policy was gradually eliminated among seamen. Despite Stevenson's efforts, however, it was not until President Truman's executive order of 1948 that discrimination on the basis of color became formally illegal in the Navy, as well as in the other armed services.

President Roosevelt's impression of Stevenson was thus formed by observation of his quiet thoughtfulness on wartime issues and of his ability to get things done by reliance on reason and persuasion. These impressions were to lead to major appointments for Stevenson in the later years of the war and in the years of settlement afterwards.

After Pearl Harbor, a Sunday on which Stevenson was reluctantly, and only at the urging of his family, away from his office on a picnic, the pace of war work accelerated. He immediately asked Secretary Knox for a commission so that he could go on active military duty. But Knox assured him that he was more useful in the post he already held. Stevenson traveled about the country a good deal, trouble-shooting at war plants, representing the Secretary at regional conferences, and visiting naval bases to deal with personnel and other administrative matters. At the end of 1942 he accompanied Knox on an inspection tour of the whole Pacific The-

ater of the war. On other occasions he visited bases in the
Caribbean and North Africa. In addition to such assignments,
Stevenson wrote most of Knox's public speeches ·and prepared
the Secretary's testimony for him when he was called before
committees of the Congress. In short, he made himself invaluable to his older friend, and Knox never lost an opportunity
to acknowledge his gratitude to his assistant.

II

IN THE LATTER PART OF 1943, after Sicily and southern Italy
had been liberated, Stevenson was appointed ˙to head a mission to Italy to determine what kinds of financial and material assistance that war-devastated country would require in
order to begin the long process of recovery and rehabilitation.
The choice of Stevenson for this important assignment shows
how high he had risen in the esteem of the President.

At forty-three Adlai Stevenson had accumulated a rich
experience of government, even though he was still looked
upon as one of the "younger men." In his work for Secretary
Knox he had not only gained close understanding of the
military departments but he had participated in the work of
such important wartime agencies as the Board of Economic
Warfare, the War Production Board, and the Office of War
Information. The latter was directed at first by Stevenson's
friend the poet Archiband MacLeish who later moved into
the State Department as an Assistant Secretary. MacLeish
was immensely impressed by Stevenson's ability and spoke to
Secretary of State Cordell Hull and President Roosevelt about
the possibility of Stevenson's being given an assignment in
foreign affairs.

When the search began for a man to head the economic
mission to Italy Stevenson was almost the first man considered. What was needed was a man who could command the
respect and cooperation of the military who were in control
of liberated Italy and who might be doubtful about a green

civilian coming so deep into a crucial war theater. At the same time the head of this mission could not himself be a military man, since the advice the President needed was not military but administrative, economic, and even political. Only a man with wide experience of government could be expected to make a reliable survey of conditions in Italy. Finally, the man selected should be able to write with such clarity and imagination that his report would be useful in all those offices of government where the problem of Italy would be considered·and would, at the same time, favorably impress the members of Congress whose cooperation would be needed in implementing the policy of Italian reconstruction. Adlai Stevenson answered so well to these qualifications that he was almost immediately recommended to the President. Mr. Roosevelt, already well disposed toward Stevenson, entrusted him with the assignment.

With a team of experts in agriculture, engineering, and economics, Stevenson left for Italy on December 7, 1943. He noted in a small diary he kept of the mission that their travels were often delayed by bad weather for flying, or by poor cooperation from military officials who resented the presence of any civilians. But Stevenson's position in the Navy frequently opened otherwise closed doors. At Algiers he was assigned to splendid quarters reserved for General Dwight Eisenhower's most distinguished guests; but he did not see the General himself at that time. A few weeks later, in Naples, the future President and his two-time opponent met in a corridor. Eisenhower inquired pleasantly after Stevenson's comfort and the facilities for his mission, but, perhaps characteristically, showed no interest in the mission itself.

Stevenson's study took six weeks of intensive travel, observation and note-taking all over Sicily and southern Italy. There were no precedents for this kind of mission, and he had, therefore, to decide on the spot what kinds of information would be most useful back in Washington when it came to policy planning. At the end of January, laden with folders of notes and documents, Stevenson and his staff set out for home. They returned by way of Liberia where Stevenson had some business for the Navy, and also a family association. His great grandfather, Lewis Warner Green, had been a member of the African Colonization Society which had sent freed negroes to Liberia in the days before the Civil War.

The report which Stevenson submitted to the Foreign Economic Administration upon his return from Italy became a model that was studied in connection with reconstruction and foreign aid for many nations. It brought its author an enviable reputation as one of the first experts in what was to become in later years one of the most far-reaching and consistent policies of the United States in the Cold War.

But Stevenson had another experience during that journey to Italy which had nothing to do with the mission itself, yet was to have greater consequence to himself and to his country than any other experience of his life. He tells the story himself in characteristic minor key:

> I think it was in Naples on a wet, cold night in that ugly winter that I naively asked Ernie Pyle [a famous war correspondent] if the G.I.'s up at the front were much interested in the soldier-vote legislation I had just been working on in Washington. He looked at me incredulously. "No," he said, "I don't think so, but I can tell you what they are thinking about. They're thinking about a dry spot where they can place their bottoms and wring out their socks." Later I went up there in the mud and blood of the Liri Valley and saw for myself.
>
> Somewhere, there in Italy, I think, I read about a public opinion poll which reported that some seven out of ten American parents disapproved their sons going into politics or public service, or something like that. From what I had already seen of war at home, in the Pacific, in the Mediterranean and from what I was still to see in Europe, I've often thought of that little morsel of news: fight, suffer, die, squander our substance, yes; but work in peacetime for the things we die for in war, no! There

seemed to me something curiously inconsistent about the
glorious, eager, uncomplaining sacrifices of war for the
security of our homeland and its cherished institutions,
and the active distaste of so many respectable people for
peacetime participation in the politics and service of that
homeland and its institutions. Die for them—yes; work
for them—no. Small wonder, I thought, that our "politics" is no better, and great wonder that it is as good as
it is. It seems to me sad that "politics" and "politician"
are so often epithets and words of disrespect and contempt, and not without justification, in the land of Jefferson and in a government by the governed.

These meditations, as he looked upon the miseries and terrors
of war there at the front in Italy, led Stevenson to resolve
that if a clear call should come to him to serve in politics, he
would heed it. Five years later, when he was asked to run for
Governor of Illinois, he responded to the urging of party leaders and personal friends. But, beyond that, he said, "perhaps
the public-opinion poll I saw in Italy had something to do
with it."

Though he returned to work for a time in the Navy Department and served for a few weeks in 1944 on the United
States Strategic Bombing Survey in the European Theater of
the War, Adlai Stevenson's service during the next few years
was to be in the field of international affairs. For three years
after the war his life was intertwined with the founding of
the United Nations and with its first heroic efforts to resolve
the tensions of the world.

Frank Knox died at the end of April, 1944, leaving Stevenson with freedom to move into other government service.
Before he left the Navy, he was awarded the highest civilian
decoration for his extraordinary services throughout the war.
For a few weeks that spring it appeared that his longtime
dream of newspaper-editing might come true and that he
would go home to Chicago. Mrs. Knox would have been
pleased to have Stevenson buy and edit the Chicago Daily
News. He organized a syndicate of friends to make an offer

for the paper. But the Stevenson group was outbid, and this last opportunity to be an editor passed him by. Later in the year he was in Europe on the Strategic Bombing Survey. But he was marking time until a major assignment in foreign affairs should turn up. In February, 1945 the moment came. He was appointed Special Assistant to the Secretary of State and assigned to work with Assistant Secretary MacLeish on a program to acquaint the American people with the need for the international organization which was soon to be launched in San Francisco.

III

IN WASHINGTON and then at San Francisco, Adlai Stevenson was not a policy-maker. His duties were, rather, to explain the work of the policy-makers to the public. This was no simple task. The basis of American policy was, at that time, co-operation with the two great wartime allies, Great Britain and the Soviet Union. Despite the heroic war effort of the Russians there was great popular distrust of communism in general and of Stalin in particular. That distrust was well justified and was fully shared by government leaders. But in view of the immense share of the Soviet Union in the victory it was impossible to proceed to reconstruction without collaboration between the Western allies and Russia. Stevenson and MacLeish had to show that a United Nations Organization including the Russians as equal partners was the best hope for future peace. Their job was made more difficult because of agreements President Roosevelt felt it necessary to make at the Yalta Conference with Stalin and Churchill, giving the Soviet Union three votes in the General Assembly (Russia, Byelo-Russia, and Ukraine), and providing for a big power veto in the Security Council. These provisions were looked upon by Roosevelt's political opponents as signs of weakness, if not "sellout" of American interests and prestige. Actually the Soviet Union had agreed to three votes for the

United States as well, but American leaders wisely decided that it would be a better demonstration of good will to the smaller nations if the claim for such extra votes was never made. It is certain, also, that the United States, regardless of which political party had been in power at the time, would have insisted on a veto in the Security Council if the Russians had not. But public opinion was divided and agitated on these and other questions as the San Francisco conference opened, and Stevenson and MacLeish worked day and night to provide the people with the necessary background for understanding United States policy.

At first Stevenson was not assigned to the delegation at San Francisco. That delegation consisted of several of the most prominent men in both the Democratic and Republican parties, under the chairmanship of the new Secretary of State, Edward Stettinius. Included were Harold Stassen, a possible Republican candidate for President in 1948, John Foster Dulles, also a Republican and an eminent international lawyer who was to be Secretary of State under Eisenhower in the 1950's, and such leaders of Congress as Republican Senator Arthur Vandenberg and Democrats Tom Connally of the Senate Foreign Relations Committee and Representative Sol Bloom of the House Foreign Affairs Committee. All of these men were used to talking directly with newspapermen about the affairs with which they were concerned. Their views on the proceedings at San Francisco sometimes differed and their interests were in fact seldom similar. Thus, though the delegation managed to hold to a fairly consistent policy, the public impression of their doings was nearly chaotic. The situation got worse rather than better, until eventually Secretary Stettinius sent for Adlai Stevenson to join the delegation as its official spokesman to the press.

Stevenson hurried to San Francisco and immediately began a series of conferences with members of the delegation to persuade them to channel their information for the public through him. His genius for showing how the best interests of the individual are best served by service to the common interest soon brought order into the press relations of the American delegation, as well as accurate news reporting. Stevenson jokingly told a friend who asked him what his job was, "I'm the official leak!"

Stevenson's role at San Francisco brought him to the attention not only of American newspapermen but of journalists from all over the world who were covering the conference. His unparalleled popularity with the world press undoubtedly dates from this period. His reputation for intelligence, frankness, and integrity was thereafter secure among some of the most influential people in the world. And to the leaders of his own country he showed not only great skill in handling the press and public opinion but such a command of the problems involved in building the international organization that he was soon appointed to the Preparatory Commission of the new United Nations which was to meet in London in November.

The London experience found Stevenson for the first time in a position of leadership. The Preparatory Commission was assigned the work of planning the structure of the operating bodies of the United Nations—the Secretariat, the Security Council, the Economic and Social Council, and the General Assembly. As Stevenson himself put it, the Commission was concerned with "putting flesh on the bare bones of the Charter." He himself was asked to join the American delegation, under Stettinius, which would attend the meetings of a preliminary executive committee charged with making recommendations to the full Commission. He accepted the assignment and, with his family, sailed for England on September 5, 1945. Thus began a career of active leadership in the United Nations which lasted through 1947, and was then interrupted until February, 1961 when Stevenson, by that time one of the best known and most highly respected statesmen of his time, returned to the UN as United States Permanent Representative.

The United Nations in the fall of 1945 was only a faint foreshadowing of the mighty force it is today. It had no buildings, no staff, no executive head—nothing, indeed, but a paper charter and a mandate to keep the peace of the world. Stevenson found the work of building the United Nations in those early days the most exciting, exacting, and rewarding work of his life. The executive committee had only just begun its work when Stettinius, the American delegation leader and the chairman of the conference, became so seriously ill that he had to withdraw entirely. Stevenson was appointed to take his place. In this position he negotiated all of the crucial issues with the British, French, Chinese, and other Allied powers, and, most important, with the Russians. The latter soon learned to respect the American diplomat for his patience, reliance on reason, and, above all, his quiet firmness. Stevenson showed them that he knew when compromise was in the common interest of the nations, but that he knew also when compromise was only yielding to bluff. He would not so yield. As chairman of the conference, Stevenson quickly won the confidence of all the powers for his fairness. Thus were hammered out agreements on the location of the future UN headquarters, on the structure of the Secretariat, on voting procedures in the General Assembly, on procedural rules for the Security Council and the Economic and Social Council, and many other matters. The work of the executive committee was so thorough and careful, and the political questions so well canvassed and resolved, at least for the time, that when the full Preparatory Commission met in November its proceedings were remarkably smooth and untroubled by East-West wrangling.

Stevenson also served as chairman of these plenary and final sessions. In the corridors and cloakrooms he worked endlessly to bring the nations to agreement on the main points of the agenda. His success brought repeated applause not only from his fellow delegates but from newspapermen. But the verdict on his achievements was not unanimous. The manner in which he handled the crucial question of locating the UN was the object of bitter attacks in the Chicago *Tribune*. That paper was never to forget Stevenson's work on the Committee to Defend America by Aiding the Allies before the United States entered World War II. During the war it had largely ignored his service to the Navy, even though he was a well-known Chicagoan. But the *Tribune* was strongly critical of the whole UN idea and soon seized upon Stevenson's role in its construction to attack him without restraint. The location of UN headquarters was a sore point for the *Tribune*. Any American who did not openly and aggressively fight to secure it for the United States was in the *Tribune's* eyes nothing less than a traitor. Stevenson's policy was to treat the application of the United States in exactly the same manner as an application from any other country. He told the Preparatory Commission that the United States would like to be considered for the UN site, but with no more claim than other nations. The *Tribune* editorialized:

> It is easy to understand why he does not want the international capitol in America. He and his kind profess an interest in foreign affairs only because they wish to get away from America and associate with foreigners, to whom they pay fawning obeisance.

The *Tribune* went on to suggest that Stevenson was "ashamed" of his roots in Bloomington, Illinois. Three years later the mighty newspaper was forced to admit grudgingly that this "traitor" had not only been elected Governor of the state, but that he had won by the largest margin in history. As for Stevenson's policy on the site of the UN, it was soon clear that his moderate and ingratiating manner and his diffidence on behalf of his country evoked a general sense of confidence which decided the delegates to award the UN site to the United States. The final vote was 30 to 14. On behalf of the United States Adlai Stevenson modestly abstained from voting.

With the work of the Preparatory Commission finished, Stevenson was asked to stay in London as senior adviser to the American delegation for the first General Assembly. In this capacity he continued his work of diplomatic negotiation behind the scenes. "I guess, I'm just a ward politician at heart," he told a correspondent of the *Christian Science Monitor*. But his achievements were of a high order. On behalf of the United States, for example, he negotiated the election of the whole slate of UN officials in three days. His success was owing, as Secretary of State James Byrnes observed, to the fact that he tried to develop a list of men who would represent not what any one nation wished but what all would find most satisfactory. When the session adjourned at the beginning of March, Byrnes wrote to Stevenson, "You have helped greatly to get the United Nations started as a going concern."

He had hardly settled back into his law practice in the summer of 1946 when President Truman appointed Stevenson to the American delegation for the second session of the General Assembly to be held in New York in the fall. Despite a pressing sense of his need to "work for his living," as he put it, Stevenson was happy to return to the UN. He had, in fact, been asked to become a permanent servant of the UN as Assistant Secretary General, but had declined because of his need for greater income to provide the best opportunities for his three growing sons. He had been asked, too, by Secretary Byrnes to be Ambassador to Brazil. And his reputation brought still other flattering offers—appointment to the Securities and Exchange Commission, among others. Such suggestions were deeply appreciated, but with considerable reluctance he resumed his law practice. Appointment as delegate to the UN, however, was welcome because it was not a full time assignment, except for two or three months at a time, yet gave him a sense of participation in the business to which he was now most devoted—building a better and safer world than that which had collapsed in the fires of the war.

In the 1946 and 1947 sessions of the General Assembly, the latter of which Stevenson also attended as an American delegate, one of the chief matters on the agenda was the disposition of the British mandate in Palestine. During World War I British Foreign Secretary Lord Balfour had promised the Jews a homeland in Palestine. But despite the heroic efforts of Jews from many parts of the world to build a new Israel out of the desert, the great powers, plagued by the counterclaims of Arabs, had been unable to agree on a final settlement of the Palestine question. After World War II, further postponement was impossible. The conscience of the world was too deeply disturbed by the terrors inflicted upon the Jews by Hitler's Nazis. The United Nations took over the problem from the British and eventually voted a statute of independence for Israel and the Arab kingdom of Jordan.

In these tense and delicate negotiations Adlai Stevenson played a major part. In particular, his patience and reasonableness helped to bring the Russians into agreement with the United States and Britain, thus molding a coalition of the great powers which could prevail in the Assembly vote. Years later, when he was a candidate for President of the United States, Stevenson was hurt by criticism from his Jewish friends that he was not a vigorous enough proponent of their cause. He was too modest to remind them of his great service to Israel in its struggle for independence. But his political supporters were less reticent. Stevenson not only succeeded in winning the friendship of Israel's Prime Minister David Ben Gurion, and of Jews everywhere, but he did so without alienating Arab opinion.

After the fall 1946 session of the General Assembly some UN correspondents were severely critical of the American performance. But no criticism was directed to Stevenson, or to Mrs. Eleanor Roosevelt whose fast friendship for Stevenson was then forming. At least one leading paper, *The Christian Science Monitor*, marked out these two for the highest praise in an article otherwise quite hostile to the American delegation. The same response followed Stevenson's performance at the 1947 Assembly. It was a satisfying experience. But when he returned to Chicago in December, 1947 he soon found that his days as a full-time lawyer and part-time diplomat were over. He was being called, now, to seek high public office. Politics was about to obtrude upon diplomacy for twelve hectic, exciting, and sometimes heroic years.

4

Governor of Illinois

I

"THE GOVERNORSHIP of a great tate," wrote Adlai Stevenson in 1953, "is an intensive education in politics, people and public administration that has few counterparts in American public life." He might well have said that it has no counterpart. It is not an accident that so many presidents and presidential candidates have been state governors. In the twentieth century President Theodore Roosevelt had been Governor of New York, President Wilson, Governor of New Jersey, President Coolidge, Governor of Massachusetts, and President Franklin D. Roosevelt had, like his cousin, been Governor of New York. President Taft had had similar experience as Governor of the Philippines. Among the defeated candidates were Taft and Theodore Roosevelt, Charles Evans Hughes who had been Governor of New York, James M. Cox who had been Governor of Ohio, and Alfred E. Smith and Thomas

E. Dewey, each of whom had been Governor of New York.
In addition, such men as Frank Lowden of Illinois, Earl Warren of California, Harold Stassen of Minnesota, and Averell
Harriman of New York, all state governors, made strong runs
for the nomination of their party. Except for dealing with
foreign affairs, a governor, especially, as Stevenson suggests,
the governor of a big state, is a kind of miniature President.
He is the chief executive of his state, commander-in-chief of
its militia, its ceremonial head, and the head of his political
party. He recommends the state's budget to the legislature
and supervises the spending of the public money after it has
been appropriated by the lawmakers. He is expected to suggest policy on nearly every matter of common interest to the
people of the state. Thus he must constantly negotiate with
the legislators, seeking not only to represent the wishes of the
people but to persuade them to accept his leadership. At first
glance it may seem that Stevenson was less well prepared for
such a post in 1948 than for a post of greater responsibility
in foreign affairs or, perhaps, in the Senate of the United
States. This was precisely what Stevenson himself thought.

Looking back on the winter of 1947-1948 Stevenson wrote
in 1953:

> When I returned to Chicago in December, 1947,
> some of the Democratic leaders asked me to run for Gov-
> ernor. This was a new departure indeed. I had never run
> for any office, had never wanted any, had never been ac-
> tive in city or state politics and knew almost none of the
> party leaders in Chicago or downstate. Moreover, 1948
> didn't look like a very good year for Democrats any-
> where, let alone in Illinois where only three had been
> elected Governor in ninety years. But I accepted. Why?
> I don't know exactly; perhaps it was because of Father
> and Grandfather Stevenson and Great-grandfather Fell
> who all had served Illinois; perhaps it was restlessness
> about settling down again after eight feverish years of war

and peace; perhaps it was the encouragement of some determined friends.

He remembered, too, his resolve as he had looked upon the battlefields in the Liri Valley of Italy. But Stevenson's recollection here conceals almost as much as it reveals. For he had in fact decided to seek office, well before he was asked to run for Governor. When personal friends of long standing, like Hermon Smith and Jane Dick, and new friends like Mrs. Eleanor Roosevelt suggested that he run for the United States Senate he was very much interested in that idea. Though he did not himself approach the Democratic leadership to see whether he could obtain the nomination, he was pleased to have others do so. And thus a boom for Stevenson for Senator was launched. It was not the first time the idea had occurred, either to Stevenson or to his friends. As far back as 1940 the possibility of Stevenson as a candidate for the Senate had been discussed. Again, during the war, there had been some mention of his going home to run for the Senate or even, in 1944, for Governor. But these developments had never got beyond the exploratory stage. Politicians were not much interested, since Stevenson was not well enough known to be an immediate political attraction; and he himself was too preoccupied with the war effort to pay more than passing attention to such suggestions.

But in the winter of 1947-1948 the situation was different. For various reasons a seat in the Senate was attractive. It would give him an opportunity to broaden his experience and usefulness in national affairs. It would provide him with a platform from which to express his ideas on foreign policy and to continue his work for international understanding and peace. His gifts as a speaker, more widely appreciated each year, would be more advantageous, perhaps, in the Senate than anywhere else.

The Illinois Democratic organization was centered in Cook County (Chicago), where for generations there had been a powerful machine better known for its ability to get out the vote than for its contributions to honest government. The organization leaders had not been people likely to move in the same circles as Adlai Stevenson. This was why earlier attempts to launch him on a political career had come to nothing. In normal times the new effort of 1948 would have had as little chance to impress the men with the power to nominate Democratic candidates.

But times were not normal. The Democratic machine, often itself accused of corruption, believed it had an opportunity to capitalize on the scandals then besetting the Republican state administration of Governor Dwight Green. To defeat Governor Green, and to win the Senate seat, candidates of impeccable reputation would be needed, men not previously identified with organization politics. And the Democratic organization had a new leader, Colonel Jack Arvey. Like Stevenson, Arvey had seen enough of the terrors and misery of war to conclude that old-fashioned ward politics was not good enough for a country whose young men could make such sacrifices. When Stevenson's name was suggested to him, Arvey was already searching for candidates who could meet the highest standards of public service. He had never heard of Stevenson, but was impressed by his record and agreed to consider him as a possible candidate for the Senate. For Governor a likely prospect was Professor Paul Douglas of the University of Chicago who at the age of 50 had enlisted in the Marines as a private, after a long career in reform political movements in Chicago. When Stevenson and Arvey finally met, the Democratic boss was sufficiently impressed by the statesman to assure him that he would be recommended to the party leadership for the Senatorial nomination.

Thus for a time it appeared that Stevenson and his friends would get their wish. "Stevenson for Senator" headquarters were opened and a working committee was formed. Presently a fund-raising campaign was begun. But then came a sudden reversal. Colonel Arvey unexpectedly notified

Stevenson that he could not, after all, have the nomination for Senator. Instead he could have the nomination for Governor. What had happened was that the party leadership had rebelled at the idea of Paul Douglas as Governor. They were simply unwilling to "reward" with the highest position at their disposal a man who had spent many years fighting them. They were willing to see Douglas go to the Senate, where party affairs would be at a minimum. But the Governor dispenses the vast patronage of state office. For that post the Democratic leadership insisted that their nominee be a man who was at least friendly to party organization and who had some sense of party loyalty. Most of the leaders did not know Stevenson personally, but they knew who he was. That is, they thought of him as the son of Lewis Stevenson and the grandson of Vice-President Stevenson. Such a man ought to have an understanding of the importance of party in American life and government. This, in effect, was the message Colonel Arvey brought to Stevenson.

At first Stevenson was seriously disappointed. He had built up enthusiasm for the Senate run, and his prospects looked reasonably good. But the governorship was quite another matter. Since his experience had been exclusively in national and international affairs, he did not feel himself well qualified. In any case, he did not wish to be governor, since in that office he would necessarily be diverted from his major interests. On the other hand, he did have a sense of the importance of party. Though he had not been active in organization politics, he was a loyal Democrat who believed that reforms of political parties ought to be accomplished by people working *in* them rather than *against* them. He now went through a period of anguished soul-searching. While his wife made no effort to influence him one way or the other, his friends, after their own disappointment, urged him to accept.

In the end Stevenson made up his mind to offer Arvey a set of conditions under which he would agree to run for

Governor. The first was that he must have a free hand to run his campaign as he chose, emphasizing those issues and policies which, in his judgment, were best for the state. This meant that the organization would have to accept him immediately as its leader. The second condition was that, if elected, no attempt whatever would be made to influence him in the making of appointments at the upper levels of the state government. Third, he told Arvey that for appointments to lower levels he would receive nominations of "deserving Democrats," but if in any instance a man suggested by the Democratic Party turned out to be less well qualified than someone else, Stevenson would reserve the right to appoint the better qualified man. After consultation with his colleagues Arvey accepted these formidable conditions, and Adlai Stevenson presently became the Democratic nominee for Governor of Illinois.

II

IN MANY WAYS Stevenson's campaign for Governor of Illinois in 1948 set the pattern for his later campaigns for President. It was an amateur operation. His purpose was to involve as many people as possible who had not previously been attracted to politics by making a campaign based upon reason and truth-telling. The gamble was that there would be enough voters in the state for whom the prospect of honest government and progressive state programs would count more than narrow self-interest, habitual party allegiance, or "pie in the sky" promises. To win, it would be necessary to detach at least some Republicans from their ticket, gain the votes of most of the independents, and hold the great majority of Democrats. Some of the latter would no doubt be lost, because there would be some district leaders who would "sit on their hands" rather than work for a candidate who promised them nothing and seemed likely to keep his promise. And there were a good many Democratic politicians, as well as Republicans, who were quite certain that 1948 was a Republican year. To work for an amateur like Stevenson would be a waste of time, or so it seemed to them.

But 1948 was a year of political surprises. In the spring various groups of Democrats, professing disappointment in President Truman, made an effort to persuade General Dwight Eisenhower to become the Democratic nominee for President. The Republicans, for their part, had already made the same attempt without success. Eisenhower, in the end, also turned down the Democrats. By the time of the convention in July all opposition to Truman had collapsed. But the liberals who had sought Eisenhower, or Justice William O. Douglas, as their candidate continued their efforts to liberalize the party by attempting to put a strong civil rights plank into the Democratic platform. Adlai Stevenson was never attracted by the moves to dump Truman. On the contrary, he felt strongly that the President's handling of foreign affairs had been courageous and correct and that he deserved another term. But he was happy to associate himself with the drive for a strong civil rights program.

At the Philadelphia convention in July, Stevenson, as candidate for Governor, was head of the Illinois delegation. He swung the delegation to Truman, acted vigorously in the civil rights struggle which alienated several southern delegations, and concluded his participation in the convention proceedings by making a seconding speech for the nomination of Alben Barkley for Vice President. Since they were distant kinsmen, it was a sentimental moment for both Barkley and Stevenson. Stevenson left the convention with many new friends in the Democratic Party. Leaders around the country were becoming aware of his charm, his adherence to principle, and his remarkable speaking ability.

Back in Illinois the campaign entered the critical stages. Stevenson had an exhausting schedule. Traveling mainly by automobile caravan, he made anywhere from two or three to six or eight speeches a day. He visited every county downstate and every ward in Chicago, some of them several times. The press was friendly, except, of course, for the *Chicago Tribune,* and so were the crowds, which grew as the campaign progressed. Though Governor Green was thought to have the edge in the earlier stages, Stevenson closed on him rapidly. Scandals in the administration were distasteful to Republicans as well as to Democrats and independents. Stevenson not only represented an opportunity for a desired change, but more and more seemed to offer an exciting challenge to lift the sights of Illinois government and life to a richer vision than people had hitherto associated with campaigning politicians.

He did not promise anything except hard work, honesty, and modernization. The latter was the heart of Stevenson's program—modernization of roads, schools, hospitals, prisons, and mental institutions. There was nothing "in it" for the greedy or the ambitious. But there was hope for everyone that the mediocrity to which Illinois had sunk could be ended—hope in proportion to the sincerity and ability of the Democratic candidate.

The measure of the confidence Stevenson won from his fellow citizens was revealed on election day. They gave him a majority of 527,067, the largest in the history of the state. At the same time Stevenson brought President Truman through in a very close race. Truman defeated Dewey in Illinois by only 33,612. Thus the election was a tribute to the personal appeal and the solid promise of Adlai E. Stevenson. During the next four years the appeal was to spread beyond the borders of the state, and the promise was to be fully realized.

III

AFTER ONLY A BRIEF VACATION following the election, Stevenson went to work, as he put it, "to learn his job," and to organize an administration which would carry out his com-

mitments to the people of Illinois. From the outset he was
encouraged by the cooperation of Colonel Arvey. The Democratic leader shielded the governor-elect from the greedy
hands of office-seekers. At the same time Arvey made it clear
to party leaders all over the state that when nominations
were made to the Governor they would have to be fully
qualified people. Thus Stevenson was free to build his cabinet without worries about party obligations, and to staff
the offices of administration, lower down, without hesitating
to reject or appoint on the basis of merit.

This happy state of affairs was unusual, if not unique, in
the modern history of the state of Illinois—and remarkable
anywhere. It enabled Stevenson to appoint a number of the
most highly qualified people in the state to posts of executive
authority, whether they were "deserving" Democrats or even
Republicans. Some, like Fred Hoehler who became Welfare
Director, were persuaded to return to Illinois from important
assignments abroad. Others left positions with much larger
salaries to answer a call to try the great experiment of good
state government. Stevenson was continually embarrassed
by the low scale of salaries available, and it took a good deal
of "selling" on his part to persuade some of the men he most
wanted to take the risk of dropping their jobs in mid-career
to join him at Springfield. One measure he took to improve
conditions was to establish a fund, from campaign contributions left in the treasury when the election was over and
from some additional gifts from friends, with which he
could make salary supplements to those whom he considered hardship cases. These men never knew the sources
of the gifts and were, therefore, never indebted to anyone
but the Governor himself, their chief. But four years
later, during the 1952 presidential campaign, efforts were
made, without success, to charge Stevenson with an illegal
private fund.

On January 10, 1949 Adlai Stevenson became the fourth
Democratic governor of Illinois since the Civil War. He had

a Democratic legislature, too. But partisanship was a good deal less important in Springfield then than the pressing need to put the state executive departments on a sound course. In a state administration that had been ridden with scandals and corruption for years, it was hard to know whom the new Governor could trust. In particular he found himself handicapped by a small state police force which had no merit or career system. The practice had always been to appoint men to the state police as a reward for political loyalty. Stevenson decided to begin his reforms with the police. He instituted a qualifying examination system, and soon professionalized the force. He now had some tools with which to work.

A pressing problem was gambling, especially in Chicago. Leaders in his own party, as well as powerful interests in Chicago, were anxious to have gambling legalized. But Stevenson opposed gambling as "the poor man's scourge." Instead of moving to legalize it, he moved to clean it up. The newly professionalized state police were ordered into the vice spots of Chicago to raid the gambling "joints." The result of Stevenson's campaign was to reduce gambling in Chicago to the lowest level of activity in history.

But the gamblers could and did retaliate. Near the top of Stevenson's list of musts, after cleaning up corruption, was a constitutional convention to revise a document which had become, in his view, entirely outmoded. At the first opportunity in the 1949 legislature, his supporters introduced a bill calling for a convention. Most of the Republican members promptly indicated their opposition to the bill. Most Democrats were for it. But it could not be passed unless all the Democrats supported the Governor. It was here that the gamblers were able to take revenge upon the Governor for his crackdown. Before the legislature were several bills to strengthen the Chicago Crime Commission—bills the Governor strongly favored. Some Democratic legislators, acting in fact as agents for the gambling interests, told the Governor that they would vote for the constitutional convention bill, thus guaranteeing its passage, if he would veto the Crime Commission bills. It was a straight "deal" of the sort previous governors had often made. Stevenson refused categorically. The Crime Commission bills became laws, but the convention bill was defeated in the lower house by the votes of two Chicago Democrats, combined with the solid Republican opposition vote. Stevenson had to be satisfied with a bill, originally proposed by the Republicans, which made it easier to amend the constitution, but eliminated the convention Stevenson had hoped for.

Over the years Stevenson's adherence to principle on the constitutional convention probably gained more for his legislative program than it lost. His opponents discovered that he was a man of his word, that he would compromise only when compromise was in the public interest, and that he would not allow party interests to interfere with the achievement of goals he shared with the people of Illinois.

IV

BUT TO HIS LASTING DISAPPOINTMENT the bipartisanship which enabled him to improve the state constitution did not extend to the field of civil rights. Several states had already enacted laws to establish fair employment practices commissions (FEPC). Stevenson felt strongly that discrimination should be eliminated by the states in order to avoid otherwise inevitable interference by the national government. He was convinced that the day of genuine equality among Americans was long past due and that the majority of the people would not much longer tolerate the kind of discrimination on the basis of color which still persisted in such fields as employment, housing, and education. An FEPC for Illinois would be a forward step of great general significance. In southern Illinois were large areas of segregation, and many employers in other parts of the State, including Chicago, commonly discriminated against negroes. The Governor had an FEPC bill introduced in the legislature and himself campaigned for it with speeches around the state and by quiet persuasion of individual legislators. But downstate Republicans were joined by some Chicago Democrats to defeat the bill every-time it was proposed.

Stevenson did not take his defeat passively. He acted by executive order to end discrimination in state employment and in contract business with the state. Long before the Supreme Court (1954) declared that discrimination in public education was unconstitutional, Stevenson gave leadership and energetic assistance to the movement to eliminate segregation in the schools of southern Illinois. And he often spoke against segregated housing.

It was in the field of housing that Stevenson's most dramatic intervention took place. In the summer of 1951 a negro family moved into an all-white community in Cicero, a small northern Illinois city adjacent to Chicago. Violence erupted almost immediately, and a serious race riot ensued. The local police made little effort to control the situation. Reporters covering the riots suggested that the police did not seem to have any strong desire to restore order. Under these circumstances Governor Stevenson decided to act. Consulting only his closest advisers and the commander of the National Guard, he made careful plans for the militia to move in. When the rioting continued despite warnings from the Governor, he declared martial law and sent in five companies of militia. Order was quickly restored. The firmness of the Governor made it clear that such behavior would not be tolerated in Illinois. There were no more such disturbances during his administration.

Stevenson's devotion to civil rights was matched by his concern for civil liberties. His administration in Illinois coincided exactly with the unfortunate "McCarthy Era" in the nation. It was a time when fear of Communism seemed to grip the minds of a great many people. Demagogues, like Senator McCarthy, played upon these fears, developing and encouraging an atmosphere of suspicion throughout the nation. In many states super-patriots led movements to combat "subversive activities" through state legislative investigations of "un-American activities," and through state laws requiring oaths of loyalty by teachers and other public servants and outlawing members of the Communist party or its "front organizations." In Illinois the legislature enacted a bill, known as the Broyles Bill, "to protect against subversive activities by making it a crime to commit or advocate acts intended to effect the overthrow of the Government of the United States or the State of Illinois." The bill outlawed "subversive organizations" and required oaths of loyalty not only of all public officials but even of candidates for public office. The bill was passed by very large majorities in both houses of the legislature and sent to the Governor with the support of such powerful organizations as the American Legion.

The Broyles Bill presented Stevenson with a hard choice —hard, that is, by ordinary standards of politics. The measure was popular. It was in tune with the times. And it was supported by organizations whose influence in elections was immense. Members of his own party in the legislature were anxious to have the bill become law, lest they be charged by the Republicans with being "soft on Communism." But Stevenson's political standards were not ordinary. After careful study of the bill he concluded that it would be harmful to the civil liberties of the people of Illinois and would contribute to rather than reduce public worries about Communism. Above all, he was convinced that the bill would be wholly ineffective against any actual subversives. Accordingly, he decided, with the proud support of his staff, to veto the bill. He composed his veto message with great care and expressed his views in vigorous, even stirring language. The document, which drew national attention, speaks the authentic voice of American libertarian democracy in such passages as these:

By such provisions as these [requiring public officials to prove their loyalty], irreparable injury to the reputation of innocent persons is more than a possibility, it is a likelihood. If this bill becomes law, it would be only human for employees to play safe and shirk duties which might bring upon them resentment or criticism. Public service requires independent and courageous action on matters which affect countless private interests. We cannot afford to make public employees vulnerable to malicious charges of disloyalty.

Does anyone seriously think that a real traitor will hesitate to sign a loyalty oath? Of course not. Really dangerous subversives and saboteurs will be caught by careful, constant, professional investigation, not by pieces of paper.

I know full well that this veto will be distorted and misunderstood, even as telling the truth of what I knew about the reputation of Alger Hiss was distorted and misunderstood. . . . But I must, in good conscience, protest against any unnecessary suppression of our ancient rights as free men . . . We will win the contest of ideas not by suppressing those rights, but by their triumph.

In quieter times, almost a decade later, the Supreme Court of the United States expressed agreement with Adlai Stevenson by declaring a similar statute in Pennsylvania unconstitutional.

But for years Stevenson himself was plagued by the Hiss matter. Alger Hiss, President of the Carnegie Endowment for International Peace and a former official of the State Department, was convicted of perjury in 1949 for having said under oath that he had not given classified government documents to a Communist agent of the Soviet Union. The two Hiss trials were among the most notorious in American history; Hiss's name became a kind of synonym for Communist subversion and espionage; and some politicians, like

Senators Joseph McCarthy and Richard Nixon, sought to undermine the reputations of public men who had had some sort of association with Hiss when the latter was in the government. Stevenson had known Hiss slightly when the two men were young attorneys in the Department of Agriculture in the early days of the New Deal. He had met him again briefly during the San Francisco conference of the United Nations. But Stevenson had never known Hiss socially and had never had more than the most casual official association with him. At the time of the acquaintance Hiss's reputation was good. He was the trusted associate of several Secretaries of State and had been elected to the Presidency of the Carnegie Endowment on the recommendation of John Foster Dulles. General Dwight Eisenhower, a member of the Carnegie board who also knew Hiss slightly, had voted for him. In 1949 Hiss's attorneys asked Governor Stevenson, along with a number of other eminent men, for a deposition to be used at the trial. Stevenson was asked simply to state the extent of his acquaintance with Hiss and to say what he knew of the man's public reputation. Stevenson responded by executing an affidavit asserting that Hiss's reputation was good at the time he had known him. Immediately he was accused by the *Chicago Tribune* and by some politicians and commentators of being "soft on Communism" and of giving aid and comfort to a traitor. Stevenson's reply was confined to pointing out that as a lawyer and a citizen he had an obligation to tell the truth when called upon in a legal proceeding. He had told the truth; if he had not done so he would have been a coward. Interest in the matter soon died out. But it was to be unhappily revived again in the midst of the 1952 presidential campaign.

V

CORRUPTION DID NOT automatically die out of the state government when Adlai Stevenson became Governor of Illinois.

There were two scandals which demanded his personal attention before the integrity of the state government was fully resorted. In one case, state meat inspectors were found to have permitted horsemeat to be sold as hamburger in return for a cut of the profits. To Stevenson's dismay an official of the state Department of Agriculture in whom he had confidence turned out to be involved in the corruption. Stevenson dismissed him, with a heavy heart and a good deal of discouragement at the difficulty of maintaining honesty in the public business. In another case the Governor received word that in some parts of Chicago cigarettes were being sold at a price so low that unless something dishonest was going on no profit could be made on them. The suspicion was that the sellers were somehow avoiding the state tax on tobacco. Stevenson quietly hired private detectives to investigate the matter. Soon it was discovered that fraudulent tax stamps were being affixed to the cigarettes by the use of stamping machines stolen from the state. This racket was wiped out and the guilty men were convicted and jailed. By the end of his term Stevenson could look back on a remarkable record of cleaning up the corruption for which the state of Illinois had been notorious under his predecessor.

But Governor Stevenson's achievements were by no means chiefly negative. In addition to vetoing undemocratic bills and putting an end to corruption he instituted some of the most constructive and imaginative reforms in the history of the state. Welfare, for example, was professionalized under Hoehler. Prisons were remodeled and prison life re- formed. Mental institutions, declared by the respected Dr. Karl Menninger to be among the worst in the country, were so improved that four years later Menninger declared them among the best. The Governor's method was to find the best man he could get to take charge of a program, regardless of his politics, and then give him unqualified support. But Stevenson would not thereafter simply turn his attention to other matters. Such things as prison reform, mental health care, assistance to education, and welfare administration received a large and continuing share of his personal attention.

In his office in the basement of the Executive Mansion he worked far into the night almost every day. When he was not at his desk he was likely to be making an inspection tour, somewhere in the state, of facilities or procedures he wished to know about at first hand. He was served by a small staff of exceptionally able young men as personal assistants, including Carl McGowan, afterwards a judge of the U.S. Court of Appeals, and William McCormick Blair Jr., later Ambassador to Denmark and the Philippines. Other young men who worked closely with Stevenson were W. Willard Wirtz, Secretary of Labor under Presidents Kennedy and Johnson, and Edward Day, Postmaster General in the Kennedy Administration. These and many others shared Governor Stevenson's enthusiasm for reform and for good government, and shared among themselves profound dedication to their chief. Their abilities and their loyalty were worth more to Stevenson, perhaps, than the support of his party. At any rate they grew with Stevenson in the respect, if not in the affection of the political leaders.

The exciting first year of Adlai Stevenson's administration in Illinois was partially blighted by domestic unhappiness. For some years Mrs. Stevenson had appeared to their mutual friends to be growing restive and unhappy over her husband's preoccupation with public affairs. She herself was chiefly interested in the arts and was something of a poet. Despite the Governor's best efforts to maintain family unity, she decided that once the children were grown she would make a separate life of her own. In the fall of 1949 Stevenson sadly announced her decision to obtain a divorce. Thereafter, his associates and friends testify, he worked so hard at his job that they feared for his health. On one occasion his sister, who often acted as his hostess in the Executive Mansion, found him in his office late at night red-eyed from fatigue. She scolded him affectionately. But he answered her gravely, "I've failed as a husband. I've failed as a father. I will succeed as Governor!" There is no need for the biographer to pry into the inner reaches of a man's private life— or his wife's—but it is worth observing that a decade later Adlai E. Stevenson, surrounded by three proud sons, was named "Father of the Year" in the United States.

However deeply sorrow might pierce the armor of Governor Stevenson, like Abraham Lincoln, his revered fellow townsman of Springfield, his humor never failed to console him and delight others. One of his veto messages, for example, became famous. He was presented with a bill to restrain cats from prowling. If this seems an unlikely kind of action for a state legislature, it is nevertheless more characteristic than not. Stevenson wisely decided that it should not be permitted to become law. One suspects that the legislators, caring less about cats than about the possible votes of bird lovers, had been quite certain that the Governor would save them from their folly. At any rate he did so, in these memorable words:

> I cannot agree that it should be the declared public policy of Illinois that a cat visiting a neighbor's yard or crossing the highway is a public nuisance. It is in the nature of cats to do a certain amount of unescorted roaming . . .

> The problem of cat versus bird is as old as time. If we attempt to resolve it by legislation, who knows but what we may be called upon to take sides as well in the age-old problems of dog versus cat, bird versus bird, even bird versus worm? In my opinion, the State of Illinois and its local governing bodies already have enough to do without trying to control feline delinquency.

As Governor, Adlai Stevenson found that he liked the human side of his job best. He liked people, and they liked him. His speeches, always polished to precision and often making use of words that dubbed their user as an "intellectual," were so effective that his political opponents could do no more than claim that Stevenson spoke over people's heads. Thus arose the famous stories about the farmer, or the cab driver, or the steel worker, or the miner—and many other kinds of people appear in various versions—who is asked whether he understood Stevenson's speech. "O yes," he says, "of course I understood every word of it, but the man in the street may have missed some of it." At hundreds of village socials, county fairs, service club meetings, ladies' clubs, and countless other places Stevenson talked to people about the business of the state, explained what the government was trying to do, and asked the people's help. He never promised more than could reasonably be carried out; often he said bluntly that something could not be done because of legislative obstruction, or because it would cost too much. And always he emphasized the responsibility of the people themselves for the conduct of their affairs. He invited, and received, an unusual degree of citizen participation in state affairs. His mail was immense, running at times to several hundred letters a day. Some of it, of course, was from carping critics or from crackpots, but the overwhelming bulk was from thoughtful citizens who had suggestions to make or offered the Governor a pat on the back.

VI

IT IS NEARLY IMPOSSIBLE to sum up in a few words the record of a state administration as vigorous, creative, and vibrant as was that of Adlai E. Stevenson in Illinois between 1949 and 1953. He himself, in his last appearance on Governor's Day at the State Fair in Springfield, in August 1952, gave as good a brief account as any:

> What we set out to do when I first talked to you from this platform as a candidate for Governor in August, 1948, we have done in three and a half short years.

*We have eliminated the useless payrollers, put state pur-
chasing on a businesslike basis, enacted a great road construction program, raised the sights of the Illinois school
system, put the state police on a professional non-political
basis, taken the Commerce Commission out of politics,
put Illinois out in front in the care and treatment of our
mental patients, amended the Constitution, extended aid
to tuberculosis hospitals, reorganized many aspects of
government, knocked out commercial gambling, enforced
the truck weight laws to protect our highways, instilled
a new sense of public responsibility among the state's
employees—and I could go on and on. And in contrast
to most all other states, we have not raised taxes for the
general purposes of the state.*

There were also things which had not been done. Education
was not yet well enough provided for by state funds; the
Constitution was still too decrepit for the middle of the
twentieth century; and many new facilities were needed,
such as prisons, hospitals, and schools. But Governor Stevenson could be forgiven for stressing in a campaign speech the
positive achievements of his administration. The desire of
his heart was for another term to complete the unfinished
business in Illinois. But when he spoke of these accomplish-
ments to the people at the fair in Springfield he was, against
his will, candidate for another office, and his life had already
entered a new and still more dramatic and creative chapter.

5

The Campaign of 1952

I

AS THE PRESIDENTIAL ELECTION of 1952 approached, Democratic leaders and newspaper columnists and editors began to show greater interest in the Governor of Illinois. While some Democrats frankly favored another term for President Harry S. Truman, it was generally recognized that, despite his courageous leadership in foreign policy, there were some serious handicaps in the way of his possible reelection. The Korean War was widely and deeply unpopular. It was hard for many, perhaps most people to understand why American soldiers had to suffer and die in so remote a part of the world for so obscure a purpose as maintaining a line between two parts of a small country against the massive armies of China. And at home there had been a shocking series of scandals involving members of the executive branch of the government, some of them close to the President personally.

No breath of scandal had touched the President himself, but he was widely criticized for poor judgment in the selection of his political associates. Under the prodding and agitating of Senator Joseph R. McCarthy many people had been led to believe, or at least to fear, that the Truman Administration was "soft on Communism" and had permitted subversives to hold responsible positions in the government. Senator Richard Nixon had made a substantial reputation by assisting in the uncovering of documents which appeared to show that Alger Hiss had been a traitor, and President Truman had fanned the political blazes thus built up by calling the Hiss affair a "red herring."

Thus for many reasons there was a search in the nation for new leadership in the Democratic Party. Some able and attractive men, like Senator Estes Kefauver of Tennessee, Mutual Security Director Averell Harriman, Vice President Alben Barkley, and Senator Richard Russell of Georgia, presented themselves to the party and the country as candidates for the presidential nomination. But their candidacies did not obscure the growing interest in Stevenson. In January, 1952, however, Stevenson filed the formal papers for his candidacy for reelection as Governor of Illinois. He had no other ambition. His desire for a second term at Springfield was frank and outspoken. He took satisfaction in the achievements of his administration, but felt strongly that much more could be done with four more years in office.

Thus it was that Stevenson was more disconcerted than flattered by the overtures made to him on January 20th by President Truman. He had gone to Washington on state business and was surprised to find a message waiting for him that the President wished to see him, apparently on an urgent matter. Stevenson and Truman (the latter in his *Memoirs*) differ a good deal in their interpretations of the meeting, but not as to the facts. Truman told Stevenson bluntly that he, Truman, had decided not to run again, that he considered Stevenson best qualified to be his successor, that an incumbent President could control the nomination of his successor, and that he was prepared to see that Stevenson received the nomination at the convention at Chicago in July.

The two men were not well acquainted personally. They had met a number of times at large political functions, at business conferences, and two or three times at small gatherings where some conversation was possible. But it was not enough for either to have fully taken the measure of the other. It seems likely that if Truman had had a better understanding of the character of Adlai Stevenson he would never have approached him with regard to the 1952 nomination. For Stevenson was not Truman's kind of Democrat. Indeed, he was not Truman's kind of man. Stevenson was introspective, sensitive, self-deprecating. His humor was witty, incisive, pointed. He saw the problems of the world and of the nation in their fullest complexity. He could not, either temperamentally or upon reflection, have confidence in simple or direct solutions of the issues which divided the world. Truman, on the contrary, was a bluff extrovert, equally at home in cabinet meeting or at the poker table. His humility was genuine but his confidence in his destiny seemed somehow to offset it. His humor was broad, and diffuse. He had little patience for the ramifications of complex problems. He ordered the atomic bomb dropped upon Japan because he was advised that it would shorten the war and save American lives. Thereafter, on his own testimony, he never missed a moment of sleep over concern as to the historical consequences of his decision. The American Presidency, as he told Stevenson, was the most powerful office in the world. It followed, in his view, that anyone whose career was cast in politics must inevitably wish to be President. He was utterly dumbfounded when Stevenson declined to run. Indeed, he was not willing to take "no" for an answer. Despite Stevenson's categorical assertion that he would not be a candidate, that he was already a candidate for Governor of Illinois, and had no further ambition, Truman broke off the conversation with the advice to Stevenson to "go home and think it over."

During the following weeks Stevenson did indeed "think it over." He was given little time to do anything else. Springfield became a mecca for reporters from national magazines and press services. Some of them simply settled in hotels to await developments. Though there had been no public statement either by the President or by Governor Stevenson after their January meeting, it was no secret. "Inside" information appeared in syndicated columns; political leaders and prospective delegates to the Democratic convention professed to know what had taken place. There was a kind of general feeling that Stevenson was being coy about the nomination, but that if the President did in fact decide to retire, the Governor of Illinois would become an open candidate. Stevenson himself did his best to ignore the stir he was creating. He missed no opportunity to declare his intentions of running for another term as Governor. And he stuck to his job as closely as he could.

But he was certainly pondering his future. He had obligated himself to talk again to Truman before the annual Jefferson-Jackson Day national Democratic dinner to be held on March 29. His concern, in the meantime, was not what he should say to the President but how he should say it, how he could explain in a convincing way his unwillingness to be a candidate for the "highest secular office in the world." In mid-March he felt that he could no longer postpone his meeting with the President. Taking elaborate precautions not to let the press know that he was going to Washington, he informed only a few close friends of his purpose. One of them, Barry Bingham, publisher of the *Louisville Courier Journal*, met him for a brief talk at the Louisville airport. Bingham, like most of his close friends, advised him not to seek the Presidency but not to close the door. To be quiet and "available" seemed to them the best course. Stevenson parted with Bingham saying, "Well, you certainly haven't been much help to me!"

In Washington, Stevenson was again offered the full support of the President, with its guarantee of the nomination, if he would announce his candidacy. Truman emphasized the importance of an early announcement so that the campaign could begin immediately. Stevenson, he pointed out, was not yet well known in many parts of the country and time would be needed for him to catch up with the Republican presidential prospects, Senator Robert A. Taft and General Dwight D. Eisenhower. The President seemed to have forgotten his earlier conversation with Stevenson. At any rate he ignored the Governor's unwillingness to be a candidate. This made Stevenson's position doubly difficult. Perhaps the coldness which afterwards developed between the two men had its origin in this second serious talk about the nomination. Perhaps it was inevitable, given the deep tempermental differences between the two men. At any rate, Stevenson quietly repeated his position: he was a candidate for Governor of Illinois and it was already too late, under Illinois law, for anyone else to file; he felt no fitness for the office of President; he had no wish to run; he would not become a candidate.

Even then Truman appears not to have been entirely satisfied that Stevenson would not change his mind. Almost as though he intended to put Stevenson in a position where he could not escape, Truman, ad-libbing during his speech at the Jefferson-Jackson Dinner, with the Illinois Governor seated in the audience, announced that he would not run for another term. Immediately afterwards the press and eager politicians surrounded Governor Stevenson. He was able to get out of the room only with difficulty. The President, for his part, was observed to be watching the scene with amusement.

But the excitement of "will he? or, won't he?" was not amusing to Adlai Stevenson. He was utterly sincere in his motives for declining to become a candidate. He felt himself too inexperienced to seek an office he revered because of its awesome potential for good or evil throughout the world. He could not understand how any man could be ambitious for such responsibility. In addition to his sense of personal inadequacy, he felt deep concern for his young sons. In the White House, it seemed to him, they would never be able to escape public attention; the separation of their parents would be constantly dramatized. Stevenson would not willingly place them in such a position. And there was his obligation to the people of Illinois. He knew that he had made good as Governor, but by that very token he owed it to the people of the state to complete the job they had assigned to him. He would not treat the Governorship of Illinois as a stepping stone to higher ambition. Finally, his view of public service, in the older American tradition coming down from Washington and Jefferson, was that the obligation to serve was not an obligation to seek. The Presidency, he felt, ought to seek the man to fill it; no man was good enough to seek it, least of all himself.

With such thoughts he sought to explain to his children and his friends his decision to take a firm course against becoming a candidate. In later years there grew up a legend of Stevenson as a modern-day Hamlet, given to indecisive brooding. This notion was, in fact, fostered chiefly by President Truman who felt that any man who would not immediately grasp a chance to be President must be constitutionally weak. It was, of course, Stevenson's very firmness and decisiveness which baffled Truman. It baffled others as well, and served Stevenson's political opponents, both in and out of his party, as a convenient weapon of attack for many years.

II

MEANWHILE THE RACE for the presidential nomination in both parties was proceeding in the spring of 1952 with more excitement and drama than had been the case for many years. In both parties there was to be new leadership, regardless of who won the Presidency. On the Republican side the early favorite was Taft. The Ohio Senator, spokesman for the conservative wing of his party, had twice previously been denied the presidential nomination. In 1952 he was making what would certainly be his last attempt to emulate his father. He was a sentimental favorite with many Republicans and many independents. But the liberal wing of the party, which had controlled the presidential nomination consistently, could not be reconciled to Taft's views on foreign policy. Though he was liberal on some issues, like public housing and education, his attitudes on international questions were isolationist, even opposed to the United Nations. Not only were these views unpopular with influential leaders of the party, they were out of tune with public opinion generally as measured by the opinion polls. There was an uneasy feeling that Taft could not win.

Under these circumstances such Republican leaders as Governor Thomas E. Dewey of New York, Republican nominee in 1944 and 1948, Senator Henry Cabot Lodge of Massachusetts, Senator Wayne Morse of Oregon, and Paul Hoffman, who had administered the Marshall Plan under Truman, sought to persuade General Eisenhower to resign his post as Commander-in-Chief of the NATO forces at Paris and come home to campaign for the Presidency.

Of Eisenhower's reluctance there can be no doubt. He had been in the presidential picture since 1946 when, in an unguarded moment, President Truman had offered to step aside in his favor in 1948. Approached by both parties in 1948 he had been forced either to make a categorical statement that he was unavailable or face the prospect of being drafted by the Democrats. He had made the statement. Like Stevenson, he had some doubts about his personal qualifications for the office and, in addition, a conviction that under any but "overriding circumstances" military men should not enter politics. In the spring of 1952 such "overriding" conditions did exist, in his opinion, in the form of Taft's candidacy. Eisenhower was a convinced internationalist in foreign affairs. He believed deeply in the United Nations and in the North Atlantic Treaty. His experience in the collective war effort of the western allies had persuaded him that only a collective effort of the same nations could preserve the peace against the new threat from the Soviet Union. On domestic matters he had few serious differences with Taft and no very deep convictions in any case. But the differences over foreign policy were so great that he could not believe that a Taft presidency would be in the best interests of the nation. And so he answered the call of the Dewey-Lodge-Hoffman-Morse wing of the Republican Party, and came home to challenge Taft. It was a close and bitter race which the General won at the Republican Convention only because his forces were able to win disputes over the seating of delegates. Taft soon recovered from his disappointment and pledged his support to Eisenhower. The Republicans presented a united front behind new leadership as Eisenhower prepared to lead what he called a "great crusade."

It has sometimes been stated, without authority, that Governor Stevenson was reluctant to run in 1952 because he saw Eisenhower winning the battle with Taft and did not believe that he could defeat the General. If Taft were to be the nominee, so the story goes, Stevenson would have been a willing candidate in the belief that he would win. Such calculations are entirely out of character. Stevenson, as we have seen, would not have been a candidate for the Democratic nomination under any circumstances. But it is an important fact that he earnestly hoped Eisenhower would win the Republican nomination. He realized that after twenty years there might well be a Republican victory. If that were to come about Stevenson felt that Eisenhower would make a much better President than Taft. And, like the General himself, he feared the effect of Taft's foreign policy views upon the nation and upon the Grand Alliance.

On the Democratic side, Senator Estes Kefauver of

Tennessee was making a spectacular run in state primaries. Capitalizing on his fame as an investigator—over television—of the national crime syndicate, the tall Tennessean combed the country looking for votes. Wearing a coonskin cap and meeting thousands of "plain folks," he formed a vivid contrast to the Democratic leaders of the Truman administration. In the New Hampshire primary, indeed, he defeated Truman by·a large margin, though the election was not a fair test of strength since Truman was entered in the contest without his consent. But Kefauver went on from New Hampshire to many other primary victories and built a long lead in delegate strength.

Primary victories, however, cannot provide a presidential candidate with enough delegates to carry a nominating convention. To win, a candidate must have the support of at least some of the big state delegations which are controlled by party leaders. Such men as Harriman and Barkley hoped to find their support in those states, while many big state leaders, like Jack Arvey of Illinois and David Lawrence of Pennsylvania, refused to endorse anyone. They preferred, they said, to wait for word from the President as to his choice. But it was evident to everyone that they were still more interested in a possible encouraging word from the Governor of Illinois.

In Chicago, despite the Governor's request that they "cease and desist," a group of Stevenson enthusiasts, including Professor Walter Johnson of the University of Chicago, were maintaining a "Draft Stevenson" headquarters. Though they had no candidate, they found delegate interest in their efforts growing up in many parts of the country. But Colonel Arvey, formally respecting Stevenson's wishes, looked upon the draft movement as a waste of time and money with no chance of success.

In Springfield, Stevenson himself tried hard to ignore the pressures and attend to state business. And he campaigned for his own renomination to the governorship. On

April 8th he was officially renominated in the Illinois primary.
A week later he acted, decisively he thought, to take himself
out of the presidential race so that the people of Illinois
would know that he was in earnest in his campaign for another term as Governor. The statement he issued seemed at
the time to bring an end to the Stevenson boom. It was un-
equivocal, yet perhaps left open the door for that rarest of
political phenomena, a genuine draft. The reader can decide
for himself how Stevenson's position in April, 1952 should
be interpreted:

> I have been urged to announce my candidacy for the
> Democratic nomination for President, but I am a candi-
> date for Governor of Illinois and I cannot run for two
> offices at the same time. Moreover, my duties as Gover-
> nor do not presently afford the time to campaign for the
> nomination even if I wanted it.
>
> Others have asked me merely to say that I would
> accept a nomination which I did not seek. To state my
> position now on a prospect so remote in time and prob-
> ability seems to me a little presumptuous. But I would
> rather presume than embarrass or mislead.
>
> In these somber years the hopes of mankind dwell
> with the President of the United States. From such dread
> responsibility one does not shrink in fear, self-interest or
> humility. But great political parties, like great nations,
> have no indispensable man, and last January, before I
> was ever considered for the Presidency, I announced that
> I would seek reelection as Governor of Illinois. Last week
> I was nominated in the Democratic primary. It is the
> highest office within the gift of the citizens of Illinois,
> and its power for good or evil over their lives is corre-
> spondingly great. No one should lightly aspire to it or
> lightly abandon the quest once begun.
>
> Hence, I have repeatedly said that I was a candidate
> for Governor of Illinois and had no other ambition. To
> this I must add that in view of my prior commitment to
> run for Governor and my desire and the desire of many

> who have given me their help and confidence in our un-
> finished work in Illinois, I could not accept the nomina-
> tion for any other office this summer. . . .

The immediate effect of this statement was to discourage
the leaders of the Democratic organization and encourage
the avowed candidates for the nomination. Stevenson activity
dwindled to almost nothing except in the offices of the draft
movement in Chicago. There, as Professor Johnson afterwards
explained, the diehards seized upon the word "could" in
Stevenson's statement. They pointed out that the statement
said that Stevenson "*could* not," not that he "*would* not"
accept a nomination for President. And so they continued
their somewhat forlorn efforts. The Governor was surprised
and perhaps a bit annoyed that these friends would not respect his clearly stated wishes.

III

WHY THEN WAS STEVENSON nominated in July? One reason,
of course, was that he remained much the best qualified man,
whether or not he was "available." Had he not fully established his high qualifications in the minds of the Democratic
leaders and of the public he would not have been nominated
despite other important considerations. But there were other
considerations. Senator Kefauver proved unable to win the
confidence of organization leaders in the big states. He was
something of a maverick, and his cries against corruption and
his calls for reform sometimes offended influential men. In
particular, President Truman felt that Kefauver was not loyal
to the Democratic Administration and refused to give him
support. Thus, though Kefauver could and did build up a
long lead in the delegate race, he could not approach the necessary majority. Another eminent candidate was Senator Richard Russell of Georgia. But though he was respected throughout the country he was too narrowly identified with the South

and with the practices of segregation to have the kind of broad national appeal a candidate must have. Senator Kerr of Oklahoma never succeeded in building up enough support to be taken seriously. This left only two candidates who might have been expected to command broad enough support among the delegates and who were, at the same time, fully qualified for the Presidency. Vice President Alben Barkley of Kentucky was one of the best-known and best-loved Americans of his time. His rich experience in government could hardly be matched by anyone in either party. But at 73, Barkley was considered by many people to be too old to undertake the Presidency. Averell Harriman, on the other hand, was in the prime of life at 60. Harriman had served the government in various high offices for many years, was equally at home in foreign and domestic affairs, and had made a brilliant record. But his reserved manner, his hesitant public speaking, and his apparent uncertainty in the tough in-fighting of nominating politics prevented him from exciting either the leaders or the rank and file delegates. He had the backing of the big New York delegation, but even they did not generate enough enthusiasm to be contagious. The fact was that many New York delegates had lost their hearts to Stevenson, and were still hoping that somehow he could be persuaded to accept the nomination.

By the time the Democratic Convention assembled in Chicago it was apparent that a deadlock among the active candidates might develop, and that a word from President Truman might, therefore, be decisive. That word came, in due course, in the form of an endorsement of Vice President Barkley. But behind the scenes the leaders of the amateur Draft Stevenson movement were serving as catalysts to bring together Stevenson supporters, who would not take the Governor's "no" as their answer, with some outstanding leaders who preferred Stevenson and were still keeping their delegate strength uncommitted. It was thus that leaders from Pennsylvania, New Jersey, Illinois, Indiana, and Ohio, as well as individual delegates from many other states, came together to make one final effort to nominate Stevenson.

Upon his arrival in Chicago, Stevenson himself made one final effort to head off a possible draft. In a plaintive speech to the Illinois delegation he asked that his name not be placed in nomination and that the delegation not vote for him. Colonel Arvey and the other delegates reluctantly agreed. It was in that speech, intended to be off the record, that newspaper men overheard Stevenson say that he did not consider himself "fit for the job—temperamentally, mentally, or physically." Afterwards he was to have those words thrown in his face many times by political opponents. The words were sincere enough, though perhaps somewhat overstated under the emotion of the moment. But the point was missed when they were taken out of the context of Stevenon's attitude toward the Presidency. He did not think *anyone* was fully "fit" for the job; therefore, he believed, the delegates should be content to find the nominee among those who aspired to it. He himself had decided to vote for Harriman.

But the frantic efforts of the leaders to reach agreements, of the candidates to put together majorities, and of Stevenson himself to avoid the nomination became insignificant after the Governor's welcoming address. So great was the enthusiasm, so inevitable the drift of the convention that Stevenson at last saw that there was no escape. He pleaded with Governor Schricker of Indiana not to place his name in nomination, but at the same time told Schricker that if nominated he would accept. Finally, as a matter of courtesy, he called President Truman in Washington to say that his name was, after all, to be placed in nomination. The President, again misunderstanding, severely reprimanded Stevenson for "not making up his mind" earlier. However, upon his arrival at Chicago the President quickly endorsed Stevenson and climbed aboard the bandwagon.

In later years Stevenson always traced his critics' charge

that he was "indecisive" to Truman's resentment that any man could at one time reject a presidential nomination only to take it later in a draft. Truman himself often claimed that there is no such thing as a draft at a presidential nominating convention, apparently never quite comprehending the fact that he had lost control of the 1952 nominating process. What is certain is that Truman did not bring about Stevenson's nomination, and so far from not being able to make up his mind, as Truman asserted, Stevenson was very firm from the beginning. It should also be recognized that he was by temperament given to weighing an action, often at some length, before making up his mind. He saw complexities and subtleties that many politicians missed (some claimed they did not exist!), and had a profound concern for the possible consequences of a decision. Thus he sometimes seemed to be uncertain and no doubt sometimes he was. It is, of course, a fair question which will be long disputed whether an effective President can afford the luxury of as much meditation as Stevenson liked to indulge in the face of crucial decisions. But it is fair to observe that over the years some rapid fire presidential decisions have had consequences which suggest that a President sometimes cannot afford *not* to ponder!

The second genuine draft of a presidential nominee in American history (the other was Garfield in 1880) took place July 26th on the third ballot. There was no deadlock; the first two ballots were necessary only because many delegates were pledged to other candidates for one or two ballots before they could switch to Stevenson. The hour was late, but the convention so obviously wanted to see and hear the new Democratic leader that he decided to go to the convention floor and make his acceptance speech. President Truman spoke first, "giving 'em hell" in his inimitable fashion, and then introduced Stevenson. The Truman speech meant that the hour of Stevenson's appearance would be very late indeed, too late for many viewers of television in the eastern and middle western states. But the contrast between Truman and Stevenson, between the old order and the new in the Democratic Party, was the more effectively dramatized for those who stayed up to listen and watch, and for the delegates themselves.

As the ovation occasioned by his appearance on the rostrum died down, the new leader of the Democratic Party spoke:

> I accept your nomination—and your program.

He was immediately interrupted by prolonged applause. He smiled and waved. But when he spoke again it was with that characteristic blend of seriousness and humor which were soon to become familiar to the nation and the world:

> I should have preferred to hear those words uttered by a stronger, a wiser, a better man than myself. But after listening to the President's speech, I feel better about myself!

The paragraphs which followed, flowing in harmony with the welcoming address of five days previous, perhaps turned more Americans into "Stevensonians"—or convinced them not to support him—than anything he afterwards did or said. At any rate his words presently took their place among the masterpieces of American political oratory:

> None of you, my friends, can wholly appreciate what is in my heart. I can only hope that you may understand my words. They will be few.
>
> I have not sought the honor you have done me. I could not seek it because I aspired to another office, which was the full measure of my ambition. One does not treat the highest office within the gift of the people of Illinois as an alternative or as a consolation prize.
>
> I would not seek your nomination for the Presidency because the burdens of that office stagger the imagination. Its potential for good or evil now and in the years

of our lives smothers exultation and converts vanity to prayer.

I have asked the Merciful Father—the Father of us all—to let this cup pass from me. But from such dread responsibility one does not shrink in fear, in self-interest, or in false humility.

So, "If this cup may not pass from me, except that I drink it, Thy will be done."

That my heart has been troubled, that I have not sought this nomination, that I could not seek it in good conscience, that I would not seek it in honest self-appraisal, is not to say that I value it the less. Rather it is that I revere the office of the Presidency of the United States.

And now, my friends, that you have made your decision, I will fight to win that office with all my heart and soul. And, with your help, I have no doubt that we will win.

After some paragraphs of tribute to other Democratic leaders and sharp criticism of the Republicans, Stevenson's main theme was a positive statement of what, as a candidate for President, he would be for:

What does concern me, in common with thinking partisans of both parties, is not just winning the election, but how it is won, how well we can take advantage of this great quadrennial opportunity to debate issues sensibly and soberly. I hope and pray that we Democrats, win or lose, can campaign not as a crusade to exterminate the opposing party, as our opponents seem to prefer, but as a great opportunity to educate and elevate a people whose destiny is leadership, not alone of a rich and prosperous, contented country as in the past, but of a world in ferment.

And, my friends, more important than winning the election is governing the nation. That is the test of a political party—the acid, final test. When the tumult and the shouting die, when the bands are gone and the lights are dimmed, there is the stark reality of responsibility in an hour of history haunted with those gaunt grim specters of strife, dissension, and materialism at home, and ruthless, inscrutable and hostile power abroad.

The ordeal of the twentieth century—the bloodiest, most turbulent era of the Christian age—is far from over. Sacrifice, patience, understanding and implacable purpose may be our lot for years to come. Let's face it. Let's talk sense to the American people. Let's tell them the truth, that there are no gains without pains, that we are now on the eve of great decisions, not easy decisions, like resistance when you're attacked, but a long, patient, costly struggle which alone can assure triumph over the great enemies of man—war, poverty and tyranny—and the assaults upon human dignity which are the most grievous consequences of each.

Let's tell them that the victory to be won in the twentieth century, this portal to the Golden Age, mocks the pretensions of individual acumen and ingenuity. For it is a citadel guarded by thick walls of ignorance and of mistrust which do not fall before the trumpet's blast or the politicians' imprecations or even a general's baton. They are, my friends, walls that must be directly stormed by the hosts of courage, of morality and of vision, standing shoulder to shoulder, unafraid of ugly truth, contemptuous of lies, half-truths, circuses and demagoguery.

The people are wise—wiser than the Republicans think. And the Democratic Party is the people's party, not the labor party, not the farmer's party, not the employer's party—it is the party of no one because it is the party of everyone.

That, I think, is our ancient mission. Where we have deserted it we have failed. With your help there will be no desertion now. Better we lose the election than mislead the people; and better we lose than misgovern the people. Help me to do the job in this autumn of conflict and of campaign; help me to do the job in these years of darkness, doubt and of crisis which stretch beyond the horizon of tonight's happy vision, and we will justify our glorious past and the loyalty of silent millions who look to us for compassion, for understanding and for honest purpose. Thus we will serve our great tradition greatly.

Just before he concluded Stevenson paid tribute to President Truman for "a lifetime of service and bravery that will find him an imperishable page in the history of the Republic and of the Democratic Party." Then he closed with a reiteration of the solemn mood in which he had commenced:

> And finally, my friends, in the staggering task you have assigned me, I shall try "to do justly and to love mercy and to walk humbly with my God."

Thus began the Stevenson era in the Democratic Party. It was a moment filled with emotion, at least to the many who were drawn to the lonely figure of the unwilling candidate. From that emotion were to spring up groups of dedicated citizens who had never before taken an active interest in public affairs—the "Volunteers for Stevenson." For the next three months such groups worked day and night to persuade others of the special quality of Adlai E. Stevenson. They argued that it was indeed "time for a change," but that Stevenson meant sharper and more creative change than did General Eisenhower. They stressed Stevenson's humility, his record of incorruptibility, his imaginative approach to great decisions and above all his reliance upon reason and the dignity of man. When he went down to defeat on November 5 a good many of these Stevensonians unashamedly wept. But what was most remarkable about their devotion was that it did not cease to be a political force after the election was lost. On the contrary, this new dedication to improving the affairs of the nation and of the Democratic Party turned out, on the part of many thousands of Stevensonians, not to be attached to the personal fortunes of their hero at all—but rather to what he stood for. In California, for example, the Volunteers for Stevenson converted themselves into Democratic Clubs, shortly after the 1952 election, and revitalized the statewide Democratic Party. Across the country in New York the Stevensonians established the Committee for Democratic Voters to do battle with Tammany Hall and reform the party. To varying degress the same sort of development took place throughout the nation.

Before the convention closed Stevenson exercised the traditional privilege of a presidential candidate to choose his running mate. After consultation with party leaders from all sections of the country and with such elder statesmen as the President, Speaker Sam Rayburn and Vice President Barkley, he chose Senator John Sparkman of Alabama as candidate for Vice President. Sparkman was a representative of the "moderate" South. That is, he was identified with liberal legislation and policies except in the field of racial discrimination. But even there he was less aggressively "Southern" than most of his senatorial colleagues from Southern states. His nomination was intended to serve as a token of Stevenson's wish to unite the party, to play up its points of agreement, rather than to emphasize its differences. In the campaign itself Stevenson was to speak as strongly for civil rights as ever Truman or Franklin Roosevelt had done, and under far more dramatic and effective circumstances, but his approach to the problem would be through rational persuasion, not divisive politics. The candidate for Vice President thus had an important role to play in the forthcoming campaign. The convention promptly nominated Sparkman and, after once more cheering Stevenson, adjourned to begin the campaign.

IV

IT IS PROBABLY still too soon to make many broad generalizations about the presidential campaign of 1952. But it is certainly safe to say that few campaigns in history generated so much enthusiasm in both parties. It is safe also to say that enthusiasm was strongest among amateurs, among people who had not previously been active in politics at all. The Volunteers for Stevenson were matched by the Citizens for Eisenhower which drew into the Republican campaign thousands of people who had formerly felt that politics was "a dirty business" and that somehow "nice people" should not get involved in it. On election day several million more people voted than had ever voted before.

Governor Stevenson, not having been a candidate until the moment he was nominated, had no campaign organization or plans. After the convention he returned to Springfield and met with his staff and a few friends to determine his course of action. He was encouraged and aided by friendly volunteers from all over the nation. Of course there were also volunteers from the Administration in Washington, but Stevenson was anxious to keep his connection with the Truman group as distant as possible. It was not so much that he lacked confidence in the President as his sense that it was time for new leadership. His own status in the party, he believed—and his chances for election—hinged in part upon his ability to show the country that he was independent, that he was making his own decisions, in short, that he was not "Truman's man." And so wherever possible he avoided giving staff appointments to Truman men. He began, indeed, by unavoidably offending the President, when he appointed a new Chairman of the Democratic National Committee, his friend Stephen Mitchell of Chicago, instead of retaining Truman's chairman. At every sensitive post in his entire organization and in the national organization Stevenson placed new faces whose interests were directed to a future that they might build with the new leader of the party, rather than toward defense of the past under Truman. Chief among these were Mitchell and Wilson Wyatt of Kentucky who became chairman of Stevenson's personal campaign staff. Stevenson's decision to establish his campaign headquarters in Springfield rather than Washington also dramatized his independence from the President—and annoyed Mr. Truman. .

Among the friends who made themselves available to help in the campaign were a number of eminent scholars and writers. Archibald MacLeish, Herbert Agar, Bernard De Voto, John Kenneth Galbraith, John Hersey, John Bartlow Martin, John Steinbeck, and Arthur Schlesinger Jr. were particularly active. Schlesinger took leave from Harvard to join the Governor's staff as chief researcher for the campaign speeches.

After what he called "prayerful deliberation," Stevenson decided to stress the following issues: patriotism and loyalty, civil rights, social welfare, relations between business and government, relations between the states and the federal government, political morality, and, above all, the Korean War and foreign policy in general. His staff set to work to collect the most relevant facts for use in connection with each topic and began to draft working papers which could be developed later into speeches. Schlesinger, with the assistance of Willard Wirtz, Carl McGowan, and David Bell, later Director of the Budget under Kennedy and of A.I.D. under both Kennedy and Johnson, and others marshalled the materials and prepared speech drafts.

As Stevenson began his speaking tours the staff quickly discovered, what his Illinois co-workers had long known, that the Governor was a new sort of politician in still another way—he insisted on writing his own speeches. Long before he was to make an appearance he would ask for the materials that had been prepared for him and then devote every available minute, pencil in hand, to re-writing, editing, correcting, and often completely altering the draft. Frequently the finished product was unrecognizable to those who had begun the work on it. Frequently, too, the candidate gave so much time to writing his speeches that there was too little time for the politicians who came to see him on his campaign train, at his headquarters, or in his hotel suites. His staff, especially men like Wyatt and Mitchell, and his confidential assistant,

William McCormick Blair Jr., tried to impress upon him the importance of the political handshake. Stevenson did not, of course, need to be told. But in his scale of values words spoken to audiences—whether to hundreds in a hall, or thousands in a public square, or millions on television—were of greater value in the process of educating and elevating the citizens than were closed door chats with party leaders anxious for favors. As Governor he had learned how easily an executive in office or a candidate can be diverted from the great business of advancing principles and policies by the lesser business of political chit-chat. He resolved not to be diverted any more than he could help. Especially as the campaign developed and became a "dialogue" between himself and Eisenhower, with daily thrust and counterthrust, he felt the pressure of time to get his thoughts in order, and gave even less of himself to visitors. He was frequently criticized for this, by President Truman among others, and it is perhaps fair to say that his speeches would have been no less effective if he had worried about them somewhat less. It was commonplace to see him, at a banquet table or on a platform in the open air or in a great hall, bent over his manuscript, pencil in hand, up to the very moment that his name was called out by the chairman of the occasion. There was undoubtedly an element of temperament as well as policy in this habit. But it could not reasonably be argued that less attention to speeches and more attention to political conversation would have won him the election. If he lost votes by offending local leaders, it was by the handful; his speeches won him votes by the thousands. At any rate, unlike those of other defeated candidates, the speeches were so well written and so thoughtful that they could and did make a best-selling book the following year.

Afterwards, in the introduction to these campaign speeches, Stevenson explained the philosophy which led him to place such emphasis on speaking instead of "politicking." "For years," he said, "I have listened to the nauseous nonsense, the pie-in-the-sky appeals to cupidity and greed, the cynical trifling with passion and prejudice and fear; the slander, the fraudulent promises, and the all-things-to-all-men demagoguery that are too much a part of our political campaigns." He resolved that win or lose his campaign for so exalted an office as the Presidency of the United States would be worthy of the office:

> Government by the consent of the governed is the most difficult system of all because it depends for its success and vitality on the good judgments and wise decisions of so many of us. But judgment and decision depend on information and understanding. In matters of public policy, candidates then have the greatest responsibility of all to inform truthfully, so that the people will understand and will have the tools of good judgment and wise decision.

The student of American government and politics will do well even today to go to Stevenson's 1952 campaign speeches and follow them through the campaign from July to November. He will find a remarkable balance of earnest and "prayerful" consideration of the principal issues of the time with effective political thrust and counterthrust, and with a liberal admixture of humor. Stevenson's humor was denounced by General Eisenhower and other Republican orators as trifling with the issues and the people. But Stevenson refused to look away from the lighter side. The plight of the world, he felt, was too serious for pompous solemnity; it was a case of genuine tragedy, and, as Lincoln had known a century before, it is the comic spirit which enables men to live with tragedy and to surmount it where circumstances make triumph possible.

Some examples of Governor Stevenson's manner of addressing his audiences may serve to suggest the tone of the whole campaign. At New York, he chose a speech to the

American Legion, at that time loudly supporting Senator Mc-
Carthy's strident attacks on presumed Communists and fel-
low-travelers in government, to make a thoughtful talk on
patriotism. "Patriotism," he said, means "a sense of national
responsibility which will enable America to remain master of
her power—to walk with it in serenity and wisdom." He
called for "a patriotism that puts country ahead of self; a
patriotism which is not short, frenzied outbursts of emotion,
but the tranquil and steady dedication of a lifetime." He
deplored the attacks made by men like Senators Jenner (Rep.,
Ind.) and McCarthy on the patriotism of General George
Marshall, "our great wartime Chief of Staff," afterwards Secretary of State and Secretary of Defense. Quoting Dr. Samuel
Johnson, he called such attacks "the last refuge of a scoundrel."
"To strike freedom of the mind with the fist of patriotism,"
he said, "is an old and ugly subtlety." He expressed his own
irrevocable opposition to Communism or any other form of
totalitarianism, but, he added, "we must take care not to burn
down the barn to kill the rats." He admonished the Legion
directly, "especially patriotic organizations like the American
Legion, must be vigilant in protecting our birthright from its
too zealous friends while protecting it from its evil enemies."
At the end the stunned audience nevertheless rose and ap-
plauded this lecture upon their dangerous shortcomings.

It was characteristic of his whole effort that Stevenson
chose Richmond, Virginia, the capital of the old Confederacy,
to speak about civil rights and discrimination. "I should justly
earn your contempt," he told his audience, "if I talked one
way in the South and another way elsewhere. Certainly no
intellectually dishonest Presidential candidate could, by an
alchemy of election, be converted into an honest President.
I shall not go anywhere with beguiling serpent words." This
meant, among other things, that he would not appeal to
Northern sentiment by unrestricted denunciation of segregation in the South. The evil of segregation he faced directly
and unequivocally, but he was quick to confess that it was to

be found everywhere in the nation, that no man had a right "to be smug on this score."

> So long as man remains a little lower than the angels, I suppose that human character will never free itself entirely from the blemish of prejudice, religious or racial. These are prejudices, unhappily, that tend to rise wherever the minority in question is large, running here against one group and there against another. Some forget this, and, in talking of the South, forget that in the South the minority is high. Some forget, too, or don't know about strides the South has made in the past decade toward equal treatment.

But understanding was not acquiescence:

> But I do not attempt to justify the unjustifiable, whether it is anti-Negroism in one place, anti-Semitism in another—or for that matter, anti-Southernism in many places. And neither can I justify self-righteousness anywhere.

On the other side of the contest it was significant that General Eisenhower, who carried four southern states, never mentioned civil rights or racial discrimination in any of his southern appearances. His avoidance of this paramount issue may well have won him votes in the election, but it assuredly cost the nation dearly when the years of tension reached their climax at Little Rock, five years later.

As the campaign developed, it became apparent that criticizing shallow patriotism before the American Legion and talking for civil rights at Richmond were not simply dramatic moments intended to catch the public eye and ear, but the deliberate pattern of the campaign. At Detroit, for example, Stevenson chose Labor Day and a huge audience of union workmen to assert that labor would get no more from his administration, if he were elected, than any other body of Americans; that the Taft-Hartley law, then the target of labor and liberal abuse, might need amending but was not, in all honesty, a "slave labor law," as so many Democratic orators were calling it. At New Orleans, he frankly stated his conviction that the tidelands off the Gulf coast were the property of the whole nation and that the rich oil reserves under the ocean should be developed for the benefit of all the people. This was in direct contrast to the popular position in Louisiana that the oil reserves should be exploited by the states under lease to private oil companies. Speaking as he did on this issue, Stevenson took issue with both of Louisiana's United States Senators, her entire Congressional delegation, and her leading newspapers. In the election he narrowly carried the state. General Eisenhower's support for the states' rights position on the offshore oil reserves certainly had a bearing on the outcome.

The same issue probably cost Stevenson the state of Texas with its 24 electoral votes. Indeed, not long after the Democratic convention Governor Allan Shivers of Texas called upon Stevenson in Springfield to seek his support for state ownership of the tidelands. Stevenson politely informed Shivers of his conviction that the national interest was paramount. Shortly thereafter Democrat Shivers switched his support to Eisenhower and led a drive to carry Texas for the General. It amused Stevenson sometimes to make a pun on the name of the Texas governor—"the Republican Old Guard," he would say, "has the shivers and the shakes." But Shivers, it appeared, had the votes.

In retrospect Stevenson believed that his campaign was on the whole successful until about the middle of October. The opinion polls showed that he was well behind at the start. This was not surprising, since he himself was not well known, while Eisenhower was a well-loved household name. But as the campaign progressed, the polls showed that Stevenson's ideas and personality were "catching on." The gap was closing. By mid-October such pollsters as Dr. Gallup and Elmo Roper found the race very close. Stevenson, never optimistic about the outcome, began to think that he might

win. On domestic issues Eisenhower was indecisive and ineffective. He castigated the Democrats for inflation, yet endorsed most of the measures and programs of the New Deal.
In the face of high prosperity and nearly full employment it
was hard for the Republicans to make much headway. Eisenhower's attacks on corruption were, of course, popular. But
despite the dramatic nature of the scandals in government
not many people were actually touched by them. And Stevenson could counter by pointing out that the scandals were exposed by the Democrats themselves and that the Democrats
were taking measures to improve government ethics. The fear
of Communism, too, was effective in the speeches of the Republican leaders. But General Eisenhower undoubtedly lost
some support when it was learned that at the request of Senator McCarthy he had deleted words of praise for General
Marshall, his mentor, from a speech in Milwaukee. And
again, it was not clear that most Americans felt themselves
directly touched by the issue of supposed Communist subversion.

What, then, was the turning point of the election? Professional analysts of the 1952 election returns are inclined to
believe that Eisenhower would have defeated Stevenson in
any case, probably by a close margin, but that his exploitation
of the Korean War during the final weeks of the campaign
made the difference between a thin and a great margin of
victory. Stevenson himself afterwards said that Eisenhower's
declaration at Detroit on October 24—"I shall go to Korea!"—
was the decisive moment. But Republicans had been hammer-
ing effectively and relentlessly on the Korean War all summer.
It was a deeply unpopular war. Many people did not understand why Americans should have to die so far from home for
so obscure a piece of earth. General Douglas MacArthur, in
his protest to President Truman, and his dismissal, had dramatized the limitations under which the army was fighting—
orders not to provoke an all-out war with China but, on the
contrary, simply to hold the line at the 38th parallel until a

truce could be negotiated. It was a complex matter, and therefore it was easy to appeal to the common desire for a quick and clear-cut solution.

Eisenhower himself had at first favored President Truman's Korean policy. But as the campaign warmed up, feelings became inflamed, and reason slid somewhat into the background. The General became deeply disturbed by Democratic claims, first made by Truman, that as Chief of Staff in 1946, he, Eisenhower, had taken the position that Korea should not be considered a defense position of the United States. The merits of this difficult military-political question were soon lost in the welter of charges and countercharges. To the Democrats it looked as though Eisenhower were betraying a position he had formerly taken in order to appeal for votes; to the Republicans it looked as though the Administration was trying to blame its unpopular war on the Republican candidate. At any rate, the General began to stress Administration mistakes, to talk of "blunders," and, finally, to suggest that the war could have been avoided before its outbreak by effective civilian leadership. "The biggest fact about the Korean War," Eisenhower asserted, "is this:

> It was never inevitable, it was never inescapable. No fantastic fiat of history decreed that little South Korea—in the summer of 1950—would fatally tempt Communist aggressors as their easiest victim. No demonic destiny decreed that America had to bleed this way in order to keep South Korea free and to keep freedom itself self-respecting.

Thus the Korean police action of the United Nations became "Truman's war," an unnecessary and tragic American blunder. The General, finally, insisted that only a new administration, headed by himself, could bring it to an end. Though his promise to go to Korea was not, in point of fact, a promise to end the war, it seemed to convey the hope that the end was in sight. Gallup and Roper polls showed that by the end of the campaign the Korean War had become the prime issue, and that General Eisenhower had all the best of it.

Stevenson, sensing the impossibility of stemming the tide the Republicans had loosed, nevertheless made every effort to counter the General's attack by patiently explaining what was involved in the war, why it had to be fought, and why there were no easy ways to bring it to an end. There was the problem of holding back Communism. This objective had been achieved by the intervention of the United Nations. The battle line had in fact been stabilized at the place where the war had begun. The position must be held until stalemate could become truce through negotiation. But what was holding up the settlement was the fate of some 50,000 Chinese prisoners held by the Americans. The Chinese command would settle if the United Nations would return the prisoners. But the prisoners wished to be free, not to go back to Communism. "If we give up on this point," Stevenson argued, "if we send these 50,000 prisoners to their death, we will no longer lead the coalition of the free world."

> With patience and restraint and with the building up of our strength the Communists will be compelled to yield, even as they yielded on the Berlin Airlift.
>
> As of the moment we have a stalemate, and stalemates are abhorrent to Americans. But let us not deceive ourselves. A stalemate is better than surrender—and it is better than atomic war. And let us not forget that a stalemate exists for our enemy as well as for ourselves.
>
> There is no greater cruelty, in my judgment, than the raising of false hopes—no greater arrogance than playing politics with peace and war. Rather than exploit human hopes and fears, rather than provide glib solutions and false assurances, I would gladly lose this Presidential election.

Stevenson in fact offered no glib solutions, and he did indeed lose the election. Eisenhower, for his part, went to Korea soon after the election. But he did not bring an end to the war, and he could not have expected to do so. Half a year later the stalemate at last became truce when, after Stalin's death, new Russian leadership persuaded the Chinese that it was not to the interests of Communism to prolong the war—and after the American negotiators had compromised the fate of the Chinese prisoners by permitting the Communists to "interview" them and thus, in some cases, blackmail them into returning to China. A year later, as Stevenson foretold, the Chinese armies, released from Korea, were available to back up the Communists of Ho Chi Minh while North Vietnam disappeared behind the Bamboo Curtain.

On the evening of November 5, 1952 the mounting returns showed plainly that Stevenson had been defeated. It was no surprise to him, and little disappointment. He had worked hard and done his best. As he looked back upon the months of incessant travel and speechmaking it seemed to him "more and more that people cared little about the issues and party records, or about precise definition of positions. They were weary of conflict, impatient and eager for repose." His thoughts went back to a "fireside chat" he had made by radio from Chicago a month before. Perhaps with a premonition of what lay ahead, he had then said:

> How long can we keep up the fight against the monster tyranny? How long can we keep fighting in Korea; paying high taxes; helping others to help ourselves? There is only one answer. We can keep it up as long as we have to—and we will.
>
> That is why we cannot lose, and will pass from darkness to the dawn of a brighter day than even this thrice-blessed land of ours has ever known.

In those words were his own faith and his distinctive quality as a public man. But on the manuscript before him was another paragraph he had to omit because his radio time was running out. The omitted words were characteristic, too, of the champion of the losing cause:

> If telling you the truth about the world as I see it
> should cause you to cast me down, and revile me, and
> with me the Democratic Party, I should still tell you the
> truth as I see it. For no office within your gift—includ-
> ing the Presidency itself—is worth the price of deception.

The voters on November 5th did indeed "cast him down,"
but they had not reviled him. As he stood before the television cameras to announce his concession of defeat his stature
was never greater:

> We vote as many, but we pray as one. With a united
> people, with faith in democracy, with common concern
> for others less fortunate around the globe, we shall move
> forward with God's guidance toward the time when His
> children shall grow in freedom and dignity in a world at
> peace.

He read a gracious telegram he had just sent to General Eisenhower:

> The people have made their choice and I congratu-
> late you. That you may be the servant and guardian of
> peace and make the vale of trouble a door of hope is my
> earnest prayer.

And then there was a word from the heart, a personal word
yet a word that spoke for the hearts of thousands of saddened
Stevensonians:

> Someone asked me, as I came in, down on the street,
> how I felt, and I was reminded of a story that a fellow-
> townsman of ours used to tell—Abraham Lincoln. They
> asked him how he felt after an unsuccessful election. He
> said he felt like a little boy who had stubbed his toe in
> the dark. He said that he was too old to cry, but it hurt
> too much to laugh.

Thus ended one of the most enlightened and moving
political campaigns in American history. But the end of the

campaign was very far from the end of the career of the loser. The stamp he had placed upon the democratic process was made of indelible ink. For the remainder of the decade American national politics and American involvement in the affairs of the world were to find in Governor Stevenson a mind and a voice of imagination and wisdom always to be reckoned with. In 1952 Adlai Stevenson had commenced a "political dialogue" with General Eisenhower and the Republican Party which commanded worldwide attention. In the years thereafter he kept the movement of ideas alive with brilliance, patience, and persistence.

6

Leader of the Opposition, 1953-1956

I

THE MONTHS IMMEDIATELY FOLLOWING the election of 1952
were almost as hectic for Adlai Stevenson as the campaign
itself had been. There was, first of all, much important unfinished business in Illinois. One pressing matter was prison
reform. In mid-October, at the height of the campaign, Stevenson had been called to Menard to deal with a dangerous
prison riot and rebellion. Desperate prisoners had captured
seven guards and held them as hostages in one wing of the
old state prison. Fortunately the prisoners were not from a
wing which housed the criminally insane. But they were
armed and were making imperious demands under threat of
shooting the hostages.

Lt. Governor Sherwood Dixon reached Stevenson by
telephone in Pittsburgh late at night following a campaign
appearance. The Governor decided to go at once to Menard

to take personal charge of the situation. Arriving by private plane just before dawn, he conferred with Dixon and prison officials. It was decided that the prisoners should be offered an opportunity to put down their arms and surrender without reprisals if they would release the hostages uninjured; otherwise the militia would go in with tear gas and guns. Against the advice of both his staff and the prison warden, Stevenson decided that as Governor he should himself take the responsibility of dealing with the prisoners. Risking assassination, he took a public address microphone into the prison yard and addressed the rebels. Quietly he told them what their alternatives were, promising only that their complaints would be fairly considered and that there would be no reprisals if they would come out and lay down their weapons. When he had finished there was a long moment of suspense—and then they came out.

The Menard episode took place at a time when there was something like an epidemic of prison rebellions taking place in various parts of the nation. Governor Stevenson and his staff searched for the underlying causes of prison disturbances in Illinois and concluded that conditions were so intolerable that the trouble could not permanently be kept down by force. Menard, for example, was a century old, had never been improved. In Stevenson's words it was a "hell hole." In the remaining weeks of his term he acted as vigorously as laws and money would permit to complete the job of prison reform. Food, shop conditions, vocational and rehabilitation facilities for prisoners, and improvement of the quality of prison staff all received the Governor's attention.

In addition to such specific problems was a great quantity of business, especially correspondence, that had accumulated during the weeks when the Governor had been away from his desk. To this accumulation was now added a daily bundle of mail which grew greater rather than less as the days passed after the election. By mid-winter Stevenson had received more than 75,000 letters about his campaign. Many of these were from supporters disappointed at his defeat, begging him to try again, and pledging to work for the ideals he had expressed in his speeches. Many were invitations to speak, before clubs, schools and colleges, political organizations, and, of course, the Democratic Party itself all over the nation.

Most remarkable among the letters, however, were many thousands from people who had *not* voted for him. There were so many of these that it almost seemed as though somewhere deep in the soul of the nation there was a bad conscience for having rejected the man who had "talked sense to the American people." These letters offered a variety of reasons for preferring Eisenhower—the Democrats had been too long in power; Eisenhower would have a better chance to clean up corruption since Democrats were the guilty ones; the Republicans must take responsibility for demoting McCarthy, which they could do only if they were in power; the Republicans must be given power so that they would once more learn how to act responsibly on foreign policy, etc. But there was a common theme of regret; many of the letters said frankly that Stevenson was the better man; nearly all expressed a wish to vote for him in the future. It is doubtful whether any defeated candidate for President ever received so much mail in the wake of his defeat. It is certain that none ever was so warmly, guiltily praised by those who defeated him. Stevenson was deeply moved as these evidences of confidence piled up. At first he attempted to send some brief word of acknowledgement personally to each correspondent, but it soon became a physical impossibility even to read the mountains of letters. However, the testimonials had their lasting effect. For, more than any other factors, the assurance that plain citizens wanted him in public life was what determined his decision to become an active leader of the opposition.

On January 8, 1953, Adlai Stevenson retired from the Governorship of Illinois. But the familiar title stayed with him. Thereafter he was always "Governor" Stevenson, even many years later when he was Ambassador to the United Nations. After leaving Springfield, he enjoyed referring to himself as "an unemployed politician." But though he held no office he was as fully employed as his energies would permit. In Chicago, with a skeleton staff, he established an office both for the practice of law when time permitted, which was seldom, and for a political headquarters which absorbed most of the time.

Stevenson's decision to be the active leader of his party until the 1956 presidential election was almost unprecedented in American political history. In the American system there is no provision for defeated presidential candidates. Whereas in parliamentary countries, like the United Kingdom, defeated leaders retain seats in the parliament and are officially recognized as Leader of the Opposition, in the United States a man who is defeated in a presidential election is expected to yield leadership, except in name, to members of his party in Congress. Even if he runs a second time he largely confines his activity to obtaining delegates during the months just preceding the next election. He is known as the "titular leader" of his party, and so recognized on formal occasions, but otherwise he is largely ignored. In 1953, however, circumstances were favorable for a departure from custom. While President Truman was the elder statesman of the party, there was no popular demand for him to act as party leader. He himself announced that he preferred to watch from the sidelines in the role of "Mr. Citizen." At the same time many leaders of the Democratic Party, as well as thousands of newly interested amateurs, urged Stevenson to capitalize on his splendid campaign and devote himself to revitalizing the party and to keeping the new administration of Eisenhower on the alert by offering thoughtful criticism and constructive alternatives of program and policy.

Various suggestions were put forward as to ways in which Stevenson could hold some sort of official position which would provide him with a platform from which to address the nation. Chief among these was the proposal that he become

Democratic National Chairman. But this post was entirely unsuited to Stevenson's needs. If he were to assume it there would have to be a wholesale reorganization of the party structure which could hardly be accomplished soon enough to be effective during Eisenhower's first term, and there would certainly be resistance to the idea in some quarters. Since other suggestions proved no better, Stevenson was left to "go it alone." He put the matter this way:

> The determining fact in my mind after the elections of 1952 was that I remained—and would remain for some time—the "titular head" of the Democratic Party. In our country this role is a very ambiguous one. . . . Yet he is generally deemed the leading spokesman of his party. And he has—or so it seemed to me—an obligation to help wipe out the inevitable deficit accumulated by his party during a losing campaign, and also to do what he can to revive, reorganize, and rebuild the party.

> Taking account of these things, I concluded to try to play my part as best I could and with some degree of planned consistency, until the shadows that await defeated candidates and titular leaders enveloped me. I enlisted a small, informal group of experts in various fields to review and critically evaluate our major public policies, most of which were of Democratic origin. I also resolved to travel extensively in order to enlarge my knowledge of the problems of a world in which the United States has preponderant power, and, therefore, responsibility . . .

Stevenson's achievement during the 1950's, remarkable on any showing, was the more so since his income from political activity was limited to minimal expenses, his staff was reduced to three or four people, and his party was united behind him only during the brief intervals of his two campaigns for the Presidency.

Despite the handicaps, Stevenson's assets were nevertheless very great. His stature as a public man and a private friend brought far more important opportunities to speak than he could possibly accept, so that he created his own platform. And he was able to command the active support of many of the nation's leading minds. During 1953 the informal advisory group to which Stevenson referred was organized by former Air Secretary Thomas K. Finletter, afterwards U.S. Ambassador to NATO under Kennedy and Johnson. Known as the "Finletter Seminar," this group included such experts on public problems as Schlesinger, Galbraith, Harriman, George W. Ball, long time close friend of Stevenson's, Paul Nitze, George Kennan, Randolph Paul, and Seymour Harris, as well as a good many other men who from time to time were brought into discussions of matters in which they had special competence. The group produced formal papers which were vigorously discussed and debated, often with Stevenson's participation. These papers were then available to him for use in public statements and speeches. The Finletter group met several times each year, serving as a kind of "shadow cabinet" to advise the "Titular Leader" in his role as very active national leader of the opposition.

II

SHORTLY AFTER LEAVING SPRINGFIELD Stevenson began to formulate plans for a world tour. His purpose was to study the areas of tension in Asia and the Middle East, and to meet with leaders and plain people in the principal nations of both the allied and the uncommitted worlds. He wished, he said, to see for himself how the massive program of foreign aid was working, how successful was the allied policy of containing Communism, and, so far as he could, to try to assess the world's future needs. Upon his return he described his mission to a Harvard University audience in these words:

> Starting from San Francisco in March, 1953, with four companions I traveled for six months around the

edges of the Communist empire through Asia, the Middle East and Western Europe. I talked to the Emperor of Japan, the Queen of England, the Pope and to all the kings, presidents and prime ministers along my route. And I also talked to countless diplomats, journalists, students, soldiers, peasants, porters, and multitudes of new and warm-hearted friends. Everywhere I encountered an eagerness to talk and a candor of expression among officials that touched and astonished me—and has heavily taxed my discretion. And often the hospitality made me wonder if my hosts were confused and thought I had been elected President in 1952!

His companions were Blair, Barry Bingham, Walter Johnson, and William Attwood, the latter then foreign editor of *Look Magazine*, which commissioned Stevenson to write a series of articles. His fees for these reports helped to defray the cost of the journey. Each of the men undertook a sort of informal assignment in each country visited. One man would devote himself to conversations with journalists, another to sounding out opposition political leaders, another would interview the country's scholars and students of public affairs. Blair was responsible for arranging Stevenson's heavy schedule of conferences, lunches, receptions, formal dinners, and frequent addresses. At the end of a long day the whole group would meet and compare their experiences. Extensive notes were kept and carefully sorted and filed. At one time Stevenson contemplated writing a book on world politics based on these rich experiences, but the demands upon his time forced him finally to discard the idea.

Upon his return to the United States, however, he gave a "Traveller's Report" over nationwide television and prepared and delivered at Harvard a course of lectures on foreign policy. These were published as *Call to Greatness* (New York: Harper and Brothers, 1954). His *Look* articles reached very large audiences and were widely quoted and reproduced. Everywhere he went on his tour, Stevenson reported, he met not only kind feelings toward himself and the country he un-officially represented, not only good will and high hopes, but also something disquieting, a deep uneasiness about the phe-nomenon known as McCarthyism. For many months after his return Stevenson, as Democratic leader, was forced to devote energy and attention to combatting this ugly symptom of po-litical disease in the American body politic.

Abroad Stevenson had been asked at every stop whether McCarthyism was as viciously anti-democratic as it seemed and why it was tolerated by the American people. Speaking as an American rather than a partisan Democrat, Stevenson answered these questions by putting the matter in the best light he could. He indicated that most of McCarthy's support came from people who agreed with his avowed purpose of ridding the government of subversives. On the other hand, he assured his interviewers that McCarthy's tactics had little sup-port. In some cases Stevenson emphasized the freedom of speech in the United States, adding that McCarthyism was a price that had to be paid for freedom.

But upon his return, Stevenson missed no opportunity to speak out against what he considered the unmitigated evil McCarthy had loosed upon the land. The issue came to its bitter climax in the winter and early spring of 1954. In Feb-ruary, Republican orators at the traditional Lincoln Day din-ners all over the country denounced the Democrats as a party of war and treason, accused them of harboring subversives, and otherwise selling out the country to the Communists. The charges were so extreme as to be ridiculous when looked at in retrospect, but they were levelled by men in high office and were taken seriously by a good many people. Even so respected a public man as Governor Thomas E. Dewey of New York, twice the Republican candidate for President, in-dulged in the extreme sort of denunciatory language which characterized McCarthyism. There were, of course, many Re-publican speakers who were quite unwilling to stoop to such irresponsible politics. But the tone of the political season was set by the loud, shrill voices of the McCarthyites. McCarthy himself had taken on the United States Army, asserting that it was infested with traitors and "soft" incompetents who did the business of the Communists. On nationwide television he was daily attacking every one from obscure noncoms to decorated generals to the Secretary of the Army himself. In Stevenson's view this disgraceful activity should long before have been brought to an end by firm presidential leadership. While President Eisenhower left no doubt that he disapproved of McCarthy, he frequently expressed himself as unwilling to tangle with him. He was content to make brief comments that he had confidence in Army Secretary Stevens or other leading men under attack from McCarthy. However, the Republican Majority Leader of the Senate, William Knowland, gave such consistent support to McCarthy that the public was confused as to the actual position of the national Republican leadership.

It was under these unhappy circumstances that Stevenson decided to speak out, as leader of the Democratic opposition, in the strongest possible language with the hope that the Republicans could be pressed to deal with their most insidious problem. At Miami Beach, March 7, addressing the Southern Conference of the Democratic National Committee, Stevenson struck with full force at the malign specter of McCarthyism:

> It is wicked and it is subversive for public officials to try deliberately to replace reason with malice; to substitute hatred for honest difference; to fulfill campaign promises by practicing deception; and to hide discord among Republicans by sowing the dragon's teeth of dissension among Americans.

Next he directed attention to the terrible consequences of unrestrained slander such as McCarthyism encouraged:

> When one party says that the other is the party of traitors who have deliberately conspired to betray America,

to fill our government services with Communists and
spies, to send our young men to unnecessary death in
Korea, they violate not only the limits of partisanship,
they offend not only the credulity of the people, but they
stain the vision of America and of democracy for us and
for the world we seek to lead.

Recalling the very fundamentals of American democracy, Stevenson showed how they were being endangered:

This system of ours is wholly dependent upon a mutual confidence in the loyalty, the patriotism, the integrity of purpose of both parties. Extremism produces extremism, lies beget lies. The infection of bitterness and
hatred spreads all too quickly in these anxious days from
one area of our life to another. And now it is also being used against distinguished Republicans. We have just
seen a sorry example of this in the baseless charges hurled
against our honored Chief Justice. And the highest officials of the Pentagon have been charged with "coddling
Communists" and "shielding treason." General Zwicker,
one of our great Army's finest officers, is denounced by
Senator McCarthy as "stupid, arrogant, witless," as "unfit
to be an officer," and a "disgrace to the uniform." For
what? For obeying orders. This to a man who has been
decorated thirteen times for gallantry and brilliance; a
hero of the Battle of the Bulge.

Stevenson summarized the general situation in these words:

Our State Department has been abused and demor-
alized. The American voice abroad has been enfeebled.
Our educational system has been attacked; our press
threatened; our servants of God impugned; a former
President maligned; the executive departments invaded;
our foreign policy confused; the President himself pa-
tronized; and the integrity, loyalty, and morale of the
United States Army assailed.

It is hard to believe, from the perspective of later years, that
there was a time when such words were no strident exaggera-

tions of what was going on in American public life, but low key statements of bitter truth. The problem, as Stevenson saw it, was to dramatize the issue and the circumstance so effectively that the Administration would have to act. He did so, to the dismay of many politically timid Democrats, by placing the responsibility for McCarthy's continuing irresponsibility directly upon the President:

> And why, you ask, do the demagogues triumph so often? The answer is inescapable: because a group of political plungers has persuaded the President that McCarthyism is the best Republican formula for success.

> Had the Eisenhower Administration chosen to act in defense of itself and of the nation which it must govern, it would have had the grateful and dedicated support of all but a tiny and deluded minority of our people.

> Yet, clear as the issue is, and unmistakable as the support, the Administration appears to be helpless. Why? . . . A political party divided against itself, half McCarthy and half Eisenhower, cannot produce national unity—cannot govern with confidence and purpose. And it demonstrates that, so long as it attempts to share power with its enemies, it will inexorably lose power to its enemies.

The speech ended upon a more inspiring if still somber note:

> I hope that we can begin to talk with one another about our affairs more seriously, moderately, and honestly, whether it be our foreign policies, or the patriotism of our people and public servants. There has been enough —too much—of slander, dissension, and deception. We cannot afford such wastage of our resources of mind and spirit, for there is important work to do which will be done together or not at all. It is for us, all of us, to recapture the great unifying spirit which still surges so strongly through the hearts and minds of America. Let

us, as Democrats, resist the ugly provocations of this hour and try to cut the pattern of America's future, not from the scraps of dissension and bitterness but rather from the full rich fabric of America's ideals and aspirations.

"Let us," in Thomas Jefferson's words, "restore to social intercourse that harmony and affection without which liberty and even life itself are dreary things," and without which, I could add, tomorrow's misfortune will mock today's expectations.

Few addresses in American history have been so effective in their immediate consequences. Stevenson had intended to put the matter so strongly that the Administration could not ignore what he said nor delay any longer the sort of vigorous action which would bring an end to McCarthyism. He succeeded. The *New York Times* put it this way:

> This speech will have to be answered by some Republican whom the people know and respect. It compels an early and definite decision on the McCarthy issue— which will be awaited with interest.

In a few days, after consultation with the President, the Republican National Committee designated Vice President Nixon to answer Stevenson. On nationwide television Nixon defended the President and the Republican Party, praising their efforts to strengthen the government and rid it of possible subversives; but then he turned to McCarthyism and, on behalf of the Republican Party, formally repudiated McCarthy:

> Men who in the past have done effective work exposing Communists in this country have, by reckless talk and questionable method, made themselves the issue. . . .

In a matter of weeks McCarthy's downfall was headlong. Before the nation in the televised hearings he appeared like a cornered man. In the Senate a motion of censure was introduced, and though it was postponed until after the fall elections, there was never any doubt that it would pass. With the disgrace of McCarthy himself, the hateful ism associated with his name faded into insignificance. The clearing of the political atmosphere was the will of a great majority of the American people. That they should get their way, "abate the thing" they didn't like, as the *New York Times* put it, was not perhaps surprising. But that the majority spokesman should have been the defeated presidential candidate, not the popular President, was a personal triumph for Adlai Stevenson as a national leader.

Stevenson's unique role, as a minority leader who nevertheless spoke on the great issues for the national majority, was confirmed by the outcome of the fall elections. At the request of individual candidates and of state and local Democratic organizations he campaigned for three months all over the nation. With the President in the background, his personal popularity not at issue, Stevenson found it possible to conduct a more effective "dialogue" with the Republicans on the chief issues before the country. On foreign policy he argued that the Administration had talked the language of "getting tough" with the Russians, yet had been cutting the defense budget and reducing the army's conventional strength in favor of a policy of reliance on nuclear weapons. This meant, said Stevenson, that the United States was less able than before to defend the interests of freedom in various spots of tension throughout the world. In domestic matters he charged the Administration with timidity in program and with weakness in currying the favor of big business. He deplored the opening of natural resources in forest lands and potential power sites on the rivers to exploitation by private enterprises.

But above all Stevenson hammered on the necessity of ridding the country of the poison of fear, fear of Communism and the more insidious fear by Americans of each other. "We believe," he said, "that it is better to discuss a question even without settling it than to settle a question without discussing it." He carried this theme from Florida to Alaska and from California to Massachusetts, winding up the campaign officially in New York City on the Saturday before election with a speech for Averell Harriman, then running for governor of of New York, and for the national Democratic slate.

The election returns gave solid proof that Stevenson spoke for the nation. The Democrats won by substantial majorities in both houses of Congress, turning out established Republicans in many areas. But perhaps most significant was that in four of the six contests where the President personally intervened to support Republicans the Democratic candidate, backed by Stevenson, was elected. As he went home to rest at his farm in Libertyville, Stevenson took satisfaction in the conviction that the Democratic victory was a repudiation of the extremism of Republican charges in the McCarthy era and a vindication of the principles of his own party for which he had stood in the contest with Eisenhower two years before. If he saw nothing personal in the results, neither a repudiation of Eisenhower nor an endorsement of himself, many others did. In particular, successful Democratic candidates for Congress and newly elected Democratic governors in many states acknowledged a direct obligation to Stevenson for coming to their assistance. His personal appearances, they believed, had made the differences between close defeat or close victory. That they would wish him to lead the party again in 1956 was a foregone conclusion.

III

THAT HE WOULD WISH to lead was, however, by no means certain. 1955 was a fateful year, for the United States and for the world. For Adlai Stevenson it was decisive. After the successful 1954 campaign he could feel that his obligations to the Democratic Party were largely met. There was money in the treasury—though never enough! The sting of the 1952 defeat had been softened by the resounding Congressional victory. Stevenson could, if he chose, gradually reduce his political activity and return to the practice of law. The 1956 presidential nomination he could leave to men like Kefauver and Harriman who were anxious to have it. There is no doubt that such a course would have been his first choice if he were let alone to decide by himself. But he was not let alone. He could not decide what course to follow without regard to the imperative demands of people and events.

Soon after the election, during the winter of 1954-1955, a frightening crisis developed in Asia, indeed two related crises. Backed by the massive Chinese armies on their northern border, the Indo-Chinese guerilla armies of Ho Chi Minh were swiftly eliminating French power in Vietnam. Perhaps as a diversionary gesture, the Chinese chose the climax of the Indo-Chinese war to strike at the offshore islands, Quemoy and Matsu, which were held by the Nationalist Chinese.

While the United States was not bound to support the French in Indo-China, though some Administration leaders were anxious to do so, the nation was bound by treaty to the defense of Formosa. Secretary of State John Foster Dulles and Admiral Radford, Chairman of the Joint Chiefs of Staff, made it clear that they wished to intervene immediately in the renewed Chinese fighting. The President appeared uncertain as to what course he should follow.

The problem was that the offshore islands were so close to the Chinese mainland—a mile or two—that sending American forces to the aid of the Nationalists there might well be intolerable provocation to the Communist Chinese. Should war break out over these islands, the Russians, bound to the Communist Chinese by a mutual defense treaty, might be called upon to take action. But the islands were not necessary to the defense of Formosa, almost a hundred miles from the mainland of China, nor was the legal position of the United States unambiguous. While Formosa had not been Chinese territory prior to World War II but had been captured from the Japanese, the islands of Quemoy and Matsu had always belonged to China. The right of the Americans to join in the defense and occupation of Formosa could not be fairly challenged, but American defense of the offshore islands would constitute intervention in the Chinese Civil War. Some Americans, impatient with the continuing tensions of the Cold War, believed that such intervention would break the stalemate and provide opportunity for an all-out attack on the Communists as the only means of ending the struggle. Others, a clear majority according to the opinion polls, thought that such a course would be mistaken. Adlai Stevenson thought it would be criminal folly.

As the crisis deepened in the spring of 1955 and the President continued to vacillate, thousands of letters, telegrams, and telephone calls came into Stevenson's Chicago law office, urging him to intervene by addressing the nation. Stevenson was troubled by conflicting feelings. He did not wish to act in such a way as to interfere with the President's conduct of foreign policy, nor did he wish to reenter the political arena. He was rather painfully aware that in the Congress almost all of his fellow Democrats were content to give the President a "blank check." Afraid that they might again be charged with being "soft" on Communism, it seemed to many of them politically expedient simply to "go along" with the popular President. Thus for Stevenson to speak out against the Administration might alienate an important segment of his own party. But he was deeply disturbed by the trend of events and fearful that reckless action by the Administration would precipitate a war in Asia which the United States would find itself fighting alone. Finally, after consultation with several informal advisors and with advance notice to the Congressional leaders of his party, he decided to speak out. On April

11, by nationwide radio from Chicago, he made an address which, like that on McCarthyism, was to have important consequences.

He began by recalling that it was just ten years since the United Nations had been founded at San Francisco with a "charter of liberation for the peoples of the earth from the scourge of war and want." But tonight, he continued:

> despite the uneasy truces in Korea and Indo-China, our country once again confronts the iron face of war—war that may be unlike anything that man has seen since the creation of the world, for the weapons man has created can destroy not only his present but his future as well. With the invention of the hydrogen bomb and all the frightful spawn of fission and fusion, the human race has crossed one of the great watersheds of history, and mankind stands in new territory, in uncharted lands.
>
> The tragedy is that the possibility of war just now seems to hinge upon Quemoy and Matsu, small islands that lie almost as close to the coast of China as Staten Island does to New York—islands which, presumably, have been fortified by the Chinese Nationalists with our approval and assistance.

Striking at Republican division on the issue, he went on:

> We now face the bitter consequences of our government's Far Eastern policy once again: either another damaging and humiliating retreat, or else the hazard of war, unleashed not by necessity, not by strategic judgment, not by the honor of allies or for the defense of frontiers, but by a policy based more on political difficulties here at home than the realities of our situation in Asia.

Since the decision rested on the President's personal judgment as to the intent of any Communist attack on the islands, it was not "improper," Stevenson said, to ask him, despite his "great military experience," whether any man "can read the mind of an enemy within a few hours of such an attack." "Is it wise," he asked, "to allow the dread question of modern war to hinge upon a guess?" He outlined the consequences of a decision to go to war in a series of questions the President must consider:

> Are the offshore islands essential to the security of the U.S.? Are they, indeed, even essential to the defense of Formosa—which all Americans have been agreed upon since President Truman sent the Seventh Fleet there five years ago?
>
> Or is it, as the Secretary of Defense says, that the loss of Quemoy and Matsu would make no significant military difference?
>
> Can they be defended without resort to nuclear weapons?
>
> If not, while I know we now have the means to incinerate, to burn up, much of living China, are we prepared to use such weapons to defend islands so tenuously related to American security?
>
> Finally, are we prepared to shock and alienate not alone our traditional allies but most of the major non-Communist powers of Asia by going to war over islands to which the United States has no color of claim and which are of questionable value to the defense of Formosa?
>
> Are we, in short, prepared to face the prospect of war in the morass of China, possibly global war, standing almost alone in a sullen or hostile world?

The questions answered themselves, and the tone of his voice, as he spoke, left no doubt as to the answers Stevenson himself would give.

The most important element in the Quemoy and Matsu peril was the risk of losing allies who could not agree to a belligerent policy by the United States. Stevenson turned next to this problem:

> I know some politicians tell us we don't need allies. Life would certainly be much simpler if that were so. But it is

not so. We need allies because we have only 6 per cent of the world's population. We need them because the overseas air bases essential to our own security are on their territory. We need allies because they are the source of indispensable strategic materials. We need, above all, the moral strength that the solidarity of the world community alone can bring to our cause. Let us never underestimate the weight of moral opinion. It was a general, Napoleon, who wrote that: "In war, moral considerations are three-quarters of the battle."

Because the great coalition, the alliance of free nations, must continue to be the basis of American foreign policy, Stevenson now proposed that a fresh start be made in dealing with the Formosa troubles by issuing a request for the advice both of "our friends" and of the "uncommitted states."

> . . . Ask them all to join with us in an open declaration condemning the use of force in the Formosa Strait, and agreeing to stand with us in the defense of Formosa against any aggression, pending some final settlement of its status—by independence, neutralization, trusteeship, plebiscite, or whatever is wisest.

Such a declaration would place the burden of responsibility for war, if war should come, squarely on the Communists, and would re-unify the free world. In addition, Stevenson proposed that the United States should ask the General Assembly of the United Nations "to condemn any effort to alter the present status of Formosa by force." This policy would repair "one of the weaknesses of our position . . . that we have been making Formosa policy as we thought best, regardless of others."

Having made his own suggestions, Stevenson next turned to a piercing criticism of the Eisenhower administration. He called for an end to "making threats" which the government "is not prepared to back up." He would not "belittle some recent achievements in the foreign field," but there is a "yawning gap between what we say and what we do." He cited the example of Indo-China, when the Vice President had "talked of sending American soldiers to fight on the mainland of Asia." This talk had ended in nothing, while half of Vietnam was lost. President Eisenhower himself had furnished a sad example of "these winged words"—his

> announcement two years ago that he was unleashing Chiang Kai-shek, taking the wraps off him presumably for an attack on the mainland to reconquer China. However, it was apparent to everyone else, if not to us, that such an invasion across a hundred miles of water by a small, over-age, under-equipped army against perhaps the largest army and the largest nation on earth could not possibly succeed without all-out support from the United States.
>
> Since it seemed incredible to sober, thoughtful people that the government of the United States could be bluffing on such a matter, the President's unleashing policy has caused widespread anxiety that we planned to support a major war with China which might involve the Soviet Union. Hence we find ourselves where we are today—on Quemoy and Matsu—alone.

As he reached his conclusion, Stevenson made an eloquent plea for patience and for unity, and for a positive attitude toward peace:

> If the best hope for today's world is a kind of atomic balance, the decisive battle in the struggle against aggression may be fought not on battlefields but in the minds of men, and the area of decision may well be out there among the uncommitted peoples of Asia and Africa who look and listen and who must, in the main, judge us by what we say and do.

He deplored "the rattling of the saber" and an American posture which "made to appear hard, belligerent, and careless

. . . those very qualities of humanity which, in fact, we value most."

As best we can, let us correct this distorted impression, for we will win no hearts and minds in the new Asia by uttering louder threats and brandishing bigger swords. The fact is that we have not created excess military strength. The fact is that compared to freedom's enemies we have created if anything too little; the trouble is that we have tried to cover our deficiencies with bold words and have thus obscured our peaceful purposes and our ultimate reliance on quiet firmness, rather than bluster and vacillation, on wisdom rather than warnings, on forbearance rather than dictation. . . .

Let this be the American mission in the Hydrogen Age. Let us stop slandering ourselves and appear before the world once again—as we really are—as friends, not as masters; as apostles of principle, not of power; in humility, not arrogance; as champions of peace, not as harbingers of war. For our strength lies, not alone in our proving grounds and our stockpiles, but in our ideals, our goals, and their universal appeal to all men who are struggling to breathe free.

Thus Stevenson cast his influence against the risk of war over Quemoy and Matsu, and for a positive approach to the world crisis. There is no doubt that, partisan though he was, he spoke for the great majority of Americans. The next day, April 12, as though he had never suggested military intervention in the islands, Secretary Dulles said that Stevenson's proposals "copied" those of the administration. "Mr. Stevenson," he said, "has in fact endorsed the administration's program in relation to Formosa." Whether the Secretary's words meant what they seemed to say or were merely politic, there is no doubt that national unity on the Formosa question followed Stevenson's speech. No more was said of going to the military defense of Quemoy and Matsu, and in the discussions of the

General Assembly overwhelming sentiment was expressed against the use of force in the Formosa Straits.

There is no reason to suppose that President Eisenhower ever personally wished to go to war over Quemoy and Matsu. And, of course, it was the Communists who preserved peace by refraining from further attack. But Eisenhower was under severe pressure from leaders of his own party and from Nationalist China. Stevenson's intervention on behalf of a peaceful solution provided Eisenhower with the unity of American opinion he required to resist these pressures. In the moment of crisis the image of Eisenhower as peacemaker seemed to waver, but it was fortified and secured by Stevenson's leadership.

Thereafter Stevenson was more than ever in the center of public affairs. While he had offended a good many members of Congress by preferring decisive policy to expedience, he had won renewed confidence from the millions of citizens who were honestly concerned at the warlike talk of Administration leaders and grateful that Stevenson had clearly presented the alternatives. The Gallup Poll showed that if he were to try for the nomination in 1956 he would win it easily, and that were he to run against Eisenhower the race would be much closer.

But Stevenson's attitude toward the Presidency was not changed by these years of party leadership and constant national and international attention. No man, he thought, should become a candidate for a presidential nomination unless there were an overwhelming demand for him to do so. The Presidency should seek its own man, and every man at all qualified should be thoughtfully assessed to see whether he would fit the dimensions of the awesome post. Stevenson knew that he was himself far better prepared then he had been in 1952, but he had no ambition to try again. If a clear and unmistakable signal should come, he would run, but he would wait for the signal.

Meanwhile he vacationed with his sons, wrote articles for national magazines and traveled abroad. Back in Illinois in July, he met with former President Truman who was in Chicago on a speaking engagement. Truman immediately raised the question of Stevenson's candidacy for 1956. If he would announce his candidacy by Labor Day, so as to get a good long start, Truman said he would give him his support. He urged Stevenson to waste no time, reminding him that in 1952 many precious months had been lost because the identity of the Democratic candidate was not determined and could not, therefore, become well enough known to counter Eisenhower's fame. But Stevenson, who seemed destined to cross the former President at every point, could not agree. For one thing, he pointed out that he was now well known throughout the nation. But more important, he was not prepared to go after the nomination in any case. If the party wanted him he would run, but the party would have to speak first. Stevenson told Truman that he expected to see all the Democratic governors the following month when the national Governors' Conference was to be held in Chicago. If these leaders of the party were clearly for him, Stevenson would consider their invitation the kind of signal for which he had been waiting. Truman, understanding Stevenson's position no better than he had in 1952, was simply annoyed. Their parting was polite enough, but it turned out to be a permanent parting of the political ways.

When the Democratic governors arrived in Chicago a few weeks later, all without exception—twenty of them—sought out Stevenson and urged him to become a candidate in 1956. It was ironic, as it turned out, that the spokesman should have been Averell Harriman of New York. "I'm with Stevenson all the way," he declared to the press. Stevenson held a reception for the governors and other state leaders at his Libertyville farm. Their warmth and enthusiasm went far beyond the kind of perfunctory endorsement that might be given to a candidate who had earned the nomination simply by loyal party activity. Despite the lingering doubts of some professionals who shared the Republican prejudice against "eggheads," Stevenson was the acknowledged leader. The epithet, attached to Stevenson during the 1952 campaign, partly no doubt because of his widening bald spot and partly because of the intellectual quality of his speeches, presently entered into the language. Stevenson himself turned it to account with his memorable quip: "Eggheads of the world unite! You have nothing to lose but your yolks!" In the summer of 1955 the great majority of Democratic leaders were not afraid of epithets. Stevenson's stature commanded not only their admiration and respect but, in many cases, their devotion.

After the Governors' Conference, Stevenson went to Central America on law business. With him he took his oldest son, Adlai, and the latter's bride. He had always followed the practice of informing his sons of his plans and asking their opinions, even when they were quite small. But now that they were maturing he consulted them in grave earnest. The trip to Jamaica and Haiti gave him an opportunity to talk over the problem of 1956 with Adlai at great length. By letter and telephone he took counsel also with Borden and John Fell. The consensus was that he should run again, though none looked forward to another defeat with any pleasure, and all feared that a defeat was just what was in store. Father and sons agreed, however, that the cause of reason and liberalism, of a consistent foreign policy of close collaboration in the Grand Alliance, and of continuing the "education and elevation of a people whose destiny is leadership" was more important than winning the election.

Upon his return Stevenson began to organize his campaign staff. To lead it he chose James Finnegan of Pennsylvania, who had been active in the 1952 draft. Willard Wirtz would direct the research and writing staff. November 19, the occasion of a National Committee fund-raising dinner in Chicago, was selected as an appropriate time to make the formal announcement of Stevenson's candidacy. The decision was conveyed to Democratic leaders in private letters or telephone calls. There was general approval and renewed enthusiasm.

There were no other candidates in view. Stevenson's nomination was certain. With a long start and a gradual build-up over the months of 1956 there would at least be a chance of convincing a majority of the voters that the Eisenhower Administration had failed in its major promises of establishing peace in the world and maintaining prosperity without inflation at home. The record showed that the new Republican leadership had not even brought an end to corruption. Eisenhower had said that anyone who served in his Administration must be "clean as a hound's tooth." But the Secretary of the Air Force had resigned under fire for using his position to assist his private business, and lesser members of the "team" had been found wanting on the same score. The Dixon-Yates contract to provide power to the Atomic Energy Commission had been exposed as a deal in which the key financial expert in the Budget Bureau was "on loan" from the finance company that arranged the terms of the contract. But in spite of the poor record of his Administration, the President's personal popularity remained amazingly high. He would be nearly unbeatable unless some unforeseen and unwanted disaster should overtake the country.

IV

THEN SUDDENLY ON September 23 all such calculations were thrown askew when President Eisenhower suffered a serious heart attack. The first reaction, when it became apparent that the President would recover, was that he could not possibly run again. In these new circumstances several ambitious Democrats decided that since the Democratic nominee in 1956 would run against Vice President Richard Nixon, not a popular man, the Democratic candidate would be likely to win. At

the Chicago Democratic dinner the first hint of what was to
come was given by Governor Harriman. Though former President Truman, known to be cool to Stevenson, praised the
latter's speech as "the best New Deal speech I've heard in a
long time," Harriman immediately attacked it. Stevenson had
pitched his address in a low key. His sense of the political
climate was that proposals sharply at odds with public expectation, as identified with Eisenhower, would at that moment
meet with so much resistance as to be sure of inadequate support. It was, he said, "an age of moderation." Under that
rubric piecemeal reforms could not only be advocated but
achieved. But Harriman saw an opening which he promptly
exploited to try to identify himself as the true "liberal" leader
of the Democratic Party. Recalling his association with Franklin Roosevelt and Harry Truman, he flatly declared that the
Democratic Party "does not know the word 'moderation.'"
Stevenson, he was suggesting, was too much like Eisenhower
and could not be expected to give the country a clear choice.
Asked whether he still supported Stevenson, Harriman said
he supported him "personally," but this did not mean that he
was committed to him for the presidential nomination. This
equivocation set the tone of the New York governor's unde-
clared campaign for many months to come.

The significance of Harriman's change of position was
not so much his own probable candidacy as its invitation to
others to challenge Stevenson. So long as no one of such
prominence in the party as Harriman or Truman was openly
criticizing Stevenson, there was no likelihood of serious primary contests to exhaust both the candidates and the party
treasury. But by mid-winter Senator Estes Kefauver had decided to try his fortunes again in all of the principal primary
states. His success in 1952, together with the opposition to
Stevenson represented by Harriman and Truman, made it appear that Kefauver could force Stevenson to choose between
testing his leadership in at least several of the primaries or
forfeiting his claim to the nomination. Kefauver calculated

correctly, and thereby wholly altered the presidential campaigns of 1956.

The new turn of events provided Stevenson with a very difficult problem. He was now faced with the hard choice of seeking the nomination by an active primary campaign, a course which would do violence to his conception both of the Presidency and of his own political role, or withdrawing his candidacy and thus shirking his responsibility to his friends and followers. His decision to accept Kefauver's challenge was arrived at after again consulting with his sons, with his advisors and friends, and with political leaders around the nation who had declared for him. Once he had made up his mind he never again looked backward—at least in public. He threw himself with all his mind and energy into the contest. But in after years he often said that had he known in the summer of 1955 what would develop by winter he would never have become a candidate at all. Indeed it is uncertain whether Harriman and Kefauver would have persisted if they had known that by February Eisenhower was to recover sufficiently to announce his intention to run for a second term.

But Stevenson had in fact become a candidate and at first, to the dismay of his friends both at home and abroad, not a successful one. The long campaign was to begin with the Minnesota primary on March 20. Stevenson had the enthusiastic support of the Minnesota leaders, Senator Hubert Humphrey and Governor Orville Freeman, and of the official Democratic organization. Confident of victory, he made several tours of the state and gave addresses in the principal cities outlining his criticism of the Eisenhower Administration. He largely ignored his contest with Kefauver, preferring to give his time and energy to challenging the Republicans rather than to debate of personal merits within his own party. Finnegan and other advisers were not at all sure that this was the way to win.

Their fears were well founded. Ten days before the Minnesota election Stevenson had a sharp warning of impending disaster. Though he had not filed in the New Hampshire primary, his name had been entered by his supporters without his authorization. The New Hampshire Stevensonians believed that their candidate would defeat Kefauver and set a pattern for the rest of the country. If Stevenson could win without campaigning the rest would be easy. But it was in New Hampshire that Kefauver had beaten Truman four years before, and the Tennessee Senator had many friends who appreciated his taking the trouble to stump the state and shake hands with the voters. The Democrats of New Hampshire on primary day gave him a great majority. The Stevenson people quickly stressed the fact that their man had not been a candidate. But after the extravagant predictions they had made beforehand this was ·not convincing. Then came the returns from Minnesota, where Kefauver had visited every hamlet and introduced himself to thousands of people who had never seen Stevenson. These Democrats, augmented by many Republicans who voted in the Democratic primary to upset Stevenson, gave Kefauver another smashing victory.* He won all but two of the state's thirty delegates, thereby knocking Stevenson out of his previously unquestioned position as the front runner for the nomination.

It was now unhappily apparent to Stevenson that he could not treat a primary campaign for the nomination as though it were part of the presidential election. Wholly different means of approach to the voters were required, if he was to continue at all. If in his disappointment he considered withdrawing, he gave no sign. At his first press conference after the Minnesota defeat he announced, "I am tired of losing elections—I don't intend to lose any more!" Asked if that meant he would do more of the handshaking that seemed to pay off so well for Kefauver, he replied with a chuckle, "Well, a certain identity *is* established between the shaker and the shakee!"

---

* Cross over was permitted under Minnesota law.

And shake hands he did, as perhaps no other presidential candidate has ever done. He crossed and recrossed all the states where his name was entered in a primary. He campaigned in every city and village in California and Florida where he was again to meet Kefauver directly. Between the Minnesota disaster and the Florida primary late in May, Stevenson won every contest—gathering into his column all the delegates from Alaska, Washington, D.C., New Jersey, Illinois, Pennsylvania, and Oregon. He rode donkeys, waved toy alligators, kissed babies, swapped yarns, ate a hundred creamed chicken suppers in a hundred different places, ate hot dogs, went to barbecues, sat with local leaders behind closed doors, and posed for thousands of pictures with every one from Indian chiefs to little league baseball players. Even the veteran Kefauver, for whom the "folksy" manner was second nature, could not match this pace. In Florida Stevenson's victory wiped out the memory of Minnesota.

V

THERE REMAINED the California primary on June 5. Stevenson was favored from the first in what was generally agreed to be the most important, because the largest, of the state primaries. But he had run into trouble on his first tour—trouble which had ominous overtones both for his own political future and for his party and the nation.

In May, 1954 the Supreme Court had declared segregation in the public schools unconstitutional. In May, 1955 the court had ordered desegregation in several southern school districts and established machinery for carrying out the decrees. President Eisenhower repeatedly refused either to give his support to desegregation measures or even to state agreement with the Supreme Court. Negroes and white opponents of discrimination were beginning to look to the Democratic candidate for President in 1956 as their spokesman.

For Stevenson civil rights thus presented a critical and

inescapable problem. While the Republicans could, as a Northern sectional party, adopt any position on civil rights they chose, the Democrats, as a national party, must somehow contain this most divisive of issues or split asunder. Stevenson, as leader of the party, had an obligation to work for party unity. His course on civil rights must be moderate, as little divisive as possible. But as a candidate for the nomination he realized that the delegates he would need for a majority at the convention in August must come from the populous states of the North ·where the election would be won or lost and where a more radical line on civil rights was demanded. His own convictions were well known and his record as a firm defender of civil rights had long been established. The question in the primary campaign was thus not so much what he believed as how he would say what he believed.

In Los Angeles, February 7, Stevenson drew groans of disapproval when he told an audience which included many Negroes that he would not, if elected, enforce desegregation of public schools by the use of federal troops. At the same time he stated his opposition to the Powell Amendment, which would have forbidden federal aid to segregated schools whether or not such schools were in defiance of court orders to desegregate. Poor schools, he continued, were themselves a major cause of racial discrimination and he could not favor keeping them poor. Someone in the audience was heard to call out, "He's a phoney." Stevenson denied emphatically that he was "appeasing the South" in order to win votes for the nomination, insisting, rather, that North and South must live together. "A Balkanized America," he said, was an "unthinkable" idea. He pleaded for understanding and patience, arguing that education would provide the only sure means of reaching peaceful solutions to civil rights questions. In a question period he was pressed to set a target date for the completion of school integration. He suggested January 1, 1963, the centennial anniversary of the Emancipation Proclamation and, significantly, the date set by the National

Association for the Advancement of Colored People. The audience in Los Angeles, however, groaned again. In sum, candidate Stevenson was not well repaid politically for his reasonableness and candor.

Stevenson and his advisors recognized that they must find some more effective way of presenting his civil rights position. Though some influential friends urged him to do so, he could not and would not change that position. But he could, perhaps, find new ways of stating it and offer some new ideas. Two important, and far reaching, ideas emerged from intensive re-study of the whole issue. A resolution, adopted by Southern members of Congress declaring that the Supreme Court had gone beyond its proper powers in the school desegregation cases, provided an opportunity for Stevenson to take a strong position. The Southern argument was that when, and if, the Court "exceeds" its authority it is proper for a state to "interpose" its sovereignty. In effect this meant to defy the national government. But the issue thus posed was clouded by the reaction of President Eisenhower who told his press conference that "interposition" was "a very vast question that is filled with argument on both sides." Stevenson, in a speech at Hartford, Connecticut, quoted Andrew Jackson's message against nullification, as interposition was known before the Civil War—"incompatible with the existence of the Union, contradicted expressly by the letter of the Constitution, unauthorized in its spirit, inconsistent with every principle on which it was founded, and destructive of the great object for which it was formed." To this ringing statement Stevenson added a firm Amen— "That was essential Democratic doctrine—and American doctrine—120 years ago. It is essential Democratic—and American—doctrine today." Thus he told his Southern Democratic colleagues where the limits of compromise might be found, and at the same time reassured his Northern supporters that patience in civil rights was not to be taken for tolerance of discrimination. Later, when asked directly what he thought of the Southern Democrats' attack on the Supreme Court decisions he replied:

> I do not agree that the Supreme Court exceeded its proper authority on school segregation. I think rather that these rulings are correct interpretations of the Constitution and the conscience of the nation.

Two days after the Hartford speech, at a press conference in New York where the Democratic Party was split between his supporters and those of Governor Harriman, Stevenson was pressed for amplification of his civil rights stand which Harriman was criticizing. He was ready with a new proposal:

> The office of President of the United States has great moral influence and great prestige and I think the time has come when that influence should be used by calling together white and Negro leaders from the areas concerned in the South to explore ways and means of allaying these rising tensions.
> Such a conference would strengthen the hands of the thoughtful and the responsible leaders of both races by whom such conspicuous progress has been made in desegregation and in maintaining good relations with the races. The prestige of the President could curb the tensions in the South. It should be exerted before the situation gets any more serious.

For his part, Stevenson repeatedly pledged to conduct such conferences and to use the influence of the Presidency should he be elected. When the idea was put to Eisenhower directly by members of Congress, the President at first vacillated, and then refused altogether. A year and a half later, after rioting had broken out in the streets of Little Rock, he did at last, too late, call such a conference. Meanwhile the federal troops, whose intervention both he and Stevenson deplored, forcibly integrated the Little Rock Central High School.

In the later stages of the primary campaign Stevenson

was seldom again challenged on civil rights. In California, where he had started so badly, he found in the end his strongest support. On June 5 the long campaign reached its climax and conclusion when Stevenson defeated Kefauver by almost two to one. In one of the most massive political victories in the history of the state, it was especially gratifying both to himself and to his staff that he carried by immense margins every district where the population was predominantly colored.

VI

AFTER CALIFORNIA Stevenson's renomination seemed certain. But despite the commanding lead the primary victories had given Stevenson, Governor Harriman nevertheless at last announced what had been evident for months, that he would be a candidate at the convention in August. Truman quickly gave Harriman his endorsement. Senator Kefauver, however, presently withdrew from the race, announced his support of Stevenson, and urged the delegates who were pledged to him to support the former Governor of Illinois. By the time the convention assembled in Chicago the only remaining doubt was the margin by which Stevenson would win the nomination.

He won, overwhelmingly, on the first ballot. The only unharmonious note of the convention was the last ditch effort of Harriman and Truman to reverse the course of Democratic history. But when the balloting was over Truman was gracious and sporting in defeat. "I am glad to have you on my side again, sir!" was the victor's cordial response.

Shortly after his nomination Stevenson addressed the convention briefly to announce a departure from precedent on the nomination of a vice presidential candidate. Instead of stating his personal preference, as was the traditional privilege of the presidential candidate, he threw the convention open. Partly this was done to underscore the fact that the Republican candidate, Nixon, was hand-picked, and partly to generate new enthusiasm among the delegates. In a dramatic contest Senator Kefauver won the nomination over young Senator John F. Kennedy of Massachusetts. The latter, in defeat, made so favorable an impression that he moved into the forefront of the Democratic Party.

On the night of August 17, 1956 all of the leaders of the Democratic Party flanked Adlai Stevenson on the platform as he once again formally took over the leadership and accepted the nomination for President. This time his manner was less diffident, his speech less defensive. His role was that of victor, and he made his hard-won claim to authority firmly felt:

> I accept your nomination and your program. And I pledge to you every resource of mind and strength that I possess to make your deed today a good one for our country and our party.
>
> Four years ago I stood in this same place and uttered those same words to you. But four years ago I did not seek the honor you bestowed upon me. This time it was not entirely unsolicited! As you may have observed. And there is another big difference. That time we lost. This time we will win!

Presently he announced the theme of the coming campaign —the New America:

> Tonight, after an interval of marking time and aimless drifting, we are on the threshold of another great, decisive era. History's headlong course has brought us, I devoutly believe, to the threshold of a New America—to the America of the great ideals and noble visions which are the stuff our future must be made of.
>
> I mean a New America where poverty is abolished and our abundance is used to enrich the lives of every family.
>
> I mean a New America where freedom is made real

for all without regard to race or belief or economic condition.

I mean a New America which everlastingly attacks the ancient idea that men can solve their differences by killing each other.

Such an America, as it turned out, was not yet to be. The moment of victory and vision at Chicago was to be followed by another, perhaps inevitable, defeat by Dwight Eisenhower, and Adlai Stevenson was never again to stand on so high a political eminence. But in defeat he was to make, paradoxically, greater contributions of program and policy than his victorious opponent—contributions that would establish him as a preeminent statesman both of his country and of the world.

7

From Presidential Candidate to
Elder Statesman: 1956-1960

I

THE CAMPAIGN OF 1956 was a long headache for the Democratic candidate, a heartache for his devoted friends and followers, and something of a disappointment to many Americans who, somewhat naively, looked forward to a repetition of Adlai Stevenson's 1952 performance. But by 1956 the conditions of life in the United States and in the world were sharply different, and so was the condition of the candidates.

Not the least of Stevenson's handicaps was that he was the first presidential candidate to run against a man in doubtful, even precarious, health. The Republican press agents had done an almost miraculous job of persuading both Eisenhower and the people that the President was fit to run again after his heart attack. Then, in the summer he suffered an acute attack of ileitis which required major surgery. But again he was officially pronounced fit. There was no doubt that his illnesses had not hurt him politically. Paradoxically, they had helped him. To his immense popularity was now added the dimension of sympathy for an aging man battling against ill health. That he could not possibly conduct the Presidency with the necessary vigor seemed of no consequence in the minds of many Americans. How could the Democratic candidate, without seeming to be unsportsmanlike, remind the nation of the almost unbearable strains upon any President? Yet the nation would pay a severe penalty for a partially immobilized President. And there was, too, the real possibility that he would not survive. In that case Richard Nixon would succeed him. While Stevenson believed that Eisenhower had failed in many essentials of leadership, he felt even more strongly that Nixon's record of demagogic activity during the McCarthy era disqualified him from the trust a people must give to their chief executive. But even to discuss such matters would seem, to some people at least, unfair campaign tactics.

As for Stevenson himself, his health was good. But he was deeply tired. By the time of his renomination, he had been campaigning continually for nine months. His body responded readily enough to rest and change of scene. But he found his mind reluctant to produce the fresh ideas and fresh modes of expression that the election itself called for. He was tired enough, mentally, to be dependent upon advisers to a degree that he had never been before.

It was in these circumstances that the so-called "new Stevenson" appeared. He himself said afterwards that he was mentally, physically, spiritually, and even financially exhausted. The "new" approach was strongly urged by his chief staff advisers, but the decision was his own. That decision was not to challenge Eisenhower more than very infrequently on foreign affairs, where the nation seemed to have confidence in him, but to try to rebuild the old Roosevelt coalition of farmers, under-privileged minority groups, and big city industrial workers around what Walter Reuther of the United

Automobile Workers had called the "gut issues,"—cost of living, unemployment, rural poverty, social security and health insurance, education, and others. All of these were real enough concerns. There had already been two recessions in Eisenhower's one term; unemployment was not declining; the farm problem was worse, not better; and no important advances had been made in the fields of health and welfare. Stevenson, calling for a "New America," could speak with deep sincerity for programs aimed to "get America moving again," as he put it in his opening speech at Harrisburg.

For a time the "new" Stevenson seemed to be making significant progress. The polls showed that he was rapidly closing the gap between himself and the President. The Democratic Party leaders were pleased and gave signs of working for the Stevenson-Kefauver ticket with greater energy than they had displayed in 1952. Senator Kefauver was an especially valuable campaigner on this kind of platform. Stevenson himself worked at it wholeheartedly. But he nevertheless found it tiresome. Important as were these domestic "pocketbook" issues, it was America's role in the world, the problem of war or peace, of freedom or communism, which engaged Stevenson's imagination. It was foreign policy, not domestic policy, which had determined him to try again for the Presidency. His speeches began to have a repetitious quality about them; they lacked the vigorous projection of the candidate's enthusiasm and commitment which had marked his great speeches four years before. And the gap between the President and the challenger, having been closed a good part of the way, began slowly to open again.

As the campaign moved into October, Stevenson's uneasiness turned into a conviction that, win or lose, he was not fulfilling the responsibilities he had undertaken so long as he did not discuss fully and candidly the matters that, whether they wished to realize it or not, concerned the American people most gravely. The atomic arms race was intensifying; in the Middle East there were dangerous intrusions of Communist arms and influence. Against the advice, even the pleading, of most of his close advisers, Stevenson at last resolved to reverse his tactics and speak out on foreign affairs.

First he tackled the question of testing nuclear weapons. Months before, at the annual meeting of the American Society of Newspaper Editors, Stevenson had proposed that the testing of hydrogen bombs be stopped; that an effort be made to persuade the Russians to agree to a permanent cessation; and that such an agreement be used as the basis for further attempts at disarmament negotiations. President Eisenhower had rejected the suggestion on the ground that testing was valuable scientifically and, in any case, necessary to American defenses. Now, in the later stages of the campaign, Stevenson reemphasized his proposal, with exciting results. Immediately the campaign came to life. "A theatrical national gesture," asserted the President. But a great many of the nation's leading scientists endorsed Stevenson's position, both because of its statesmanship and because evidence had developed that fallout from massive explosions was poisoning the atmosphere with a cancer-producing element, Strontium 90. Willard Libby, Chairman of the Atomic Energy Commission, came to Eisenhower's support by belittling the significance of this evidence. A battle of scientists followed. A large majority supported Stevenson. The principal inventor of the H-bomb, Edward Teller, sided with the President. Both sides produced and published "white papers" intended to document the rival positions with military and scientific evidence. The polls showed that the Republican side had the best of the issue. To a majority of the people it seemed like a military question; they were prepared to trust the judgment of the general against the claims of the civilian. But Stevenson's constructive, often fervent, handling of the controversy did much to restore his "image" and prestige among his 1952 admirers. In speeches on October 15 and 17 he was at his best:

> . . . I say to you that leaders must lead; that where the
> issue is of such magnitude, I have no right to stand si-
> lent; I owe it to you to express my views, whatever the
> consequences.
>
> I repeat: this step can be taken. We can break the
> deadlock. We can make a fresh start. We can put the
> world on a new path to peace.

Stevenson's position was badly distorted both by the press and by the Republicans. While he had called for cessation of H-bomb testing without inspection, since none would be needed for detection, he had said nothing about the testing of smaller weapons. That matter he left to be dealt with after the deadlock had been broken. But Eisenhower and other Republican orators insisted on making it appear that Stevenson wished to stop *all* tests without inspection. For this he was charged at worst with "criminal irresponsibility," at best with "folly." Neither Stevenson nor his anxious staff could know that inside of two years his position on the bomb would be confirmed and adopted by the Administration— two years too late. At the moment, in 1956, it looked as though a very high price indeed were being paid for being "right" rather than President.

And as if Stevenson had not, by his courageous insistence on an unpopular stand, made matters sufficiently difficult for himself, Chairman Bulganin of the Soviet Union chose this moment, October 21, to interfere in the American election in outrageous fashion. In a letter to President Eisenhower, he called attention to Stevenson's proposals, ("certain prominent figures"). The Soviet Union, he asserted, was prepared "to conclude an agreement with the United States of America for immediately discontinuing atomic tests." It was crude enough to write such a letter at all in the midst of an election campaign, and was no doubt intended to cause disruption. But Bulganin, deliberately, made it appear that Stevenson's proposal called for an end to all testing without inspection. Under the circumstances there was little that the Democratic candidate could do but issue a strong statement supporting the President's rejection of the Bulganin letter as, in Eisenhower's words, "an interference by a foreign nation in our internal affairs of a kind which, if indulged in by an Ambassador, would lead to his being declared *persona non grata* in accordance with long established custom." Stevenson entirely agreed with this sentiment. But he could not in conscience stop there. The President's rejection of the Russian overture might be diplomatically and politically right, but it might also be historically mistaken. In his statement, therefore, Stevenson said:

> The real issue is what we are going to do to save the world from hydrogen disaster. Viewed from the standpoint, not of politics, but of peace, I think the President's reply is unfortunate.

"There are two possibilities," he continued:

> One is that Bulganin's offer is made for propaganda purposes only . . . if that is true, it should be exposed for all the world to see. The other possibility is that the Russian offer, ill-timed as it is, reflects an opportunity to move ahead now toward a stop to the further explosion of hydrogen bombs. In either event, there seems to me only one course to follow. That is to pursue this opening immediately and all the way.

There is, of course, no way of knowing whether a positive response by the United States at that time would have opened an era of fruitful negotiations. What is certain is that before another year had passed the Administration was admitting the danger of fallout, calling for an end to testing, and drastically reducing its minimum demands for inspection to detect even small explosions. Seven years later, in another era of American history, Stevenson had the satisfaction of serving in an Administration which in fact negotiated and signed a far-reaching ban on nuclear testing nearly identical with his own original proposals. In October 1956, however, it was apparent that he was fighting a losing battle.

The second theme Stevenson decided to stress in the closing stages of the campaign was American policy in the Middle East. As early as 1953 and 1954 he had expressed his view that the United States should sell arms to Israel, in 'order to prevent the development of military imbalance between the Israelis and the Arabs. As one of the principal architects of the act of the United Nations which gave Israel independence, Stevenson had always been a warm friend and supporter of Jewish hopes and dreams. He reacted sharply when the Eisenhower Administration made overtures to Nasser in Egypt while rejecting Israel's request for arms. As the Israeli-Arab border clashes continued in 1955, Stevenson proposed, at Charlottesville, Virginia, November 11, that the United Nations establish a police force to maintain peace in the area:

> A major effort of statesmanship is required if we are to avert a political disaster in this troubled area. We have shown little initiative within or outside the United Nations in devising measures to prevent these border clashes. After years of experience it would seem evident that the only way to avoid bloodshed and violence along the border is to keep the troops of these antagonists apart. And I wonder if United Nations guards could not undertake patrol duties in the area of tension and collision. Certainly both sides would respect United Nations patrols where they do not trust each other.

But the Administration rejected the plan. Indeed, without our directly saying so at any time, the Administration seemed to favor the build-up of Arab strength. The effect of its policy was to discriminate against Israel. The Egyptians and other Arab leaders talked of destroying Israel in a renewed war in the Middle East, while some Israeli leaders threatened a "preventive war" against the Arabs before they were too heavily armed. As a gesture of good will toward the Arab world, the Eisenhower Administration even persuaded the British to withdraw their troops from the Suez Canal area several years in advance of the expiration of the Canal Treaty.

In April, 1956, President Eisenhower had boasted before the American Society of Newspaper Editors that the world was moving toward peace. He cited the Middle East as an example of the general improvement of conditions, despite the fact that there were almost daily border incidents in which Arabs and Jews were killed and ignoring the evident fact that Israel's patience was becoming exhausted. On the same day Stevenson, in the address in which he called for an end to H-bomb testing, had asserted that the world was not nearer peace, that the Middle East was a dangerous area, and that the United States and the West were losing the Cold War. The editors, in an informal poll, agreed with Stevenson's analysis of the situation, not with the President's.

Later in the year, when the Egyptians accepted shipments of arms from the Communist bloc, the United States withheld funds previously promised for the construction of the Aswan Dam on the Nile. Egypt retaliated by taking over the Suez Canal. Over and over again in 1956 Stevenson had deplored the precipitate action of the American government. He called for patience, for ending the arms race in the Middle East, or at least maintaining the balance of arms until the race could be stopped, and urged a creative approach to the whole area through such cooperative development projects as a Jordan Valley Authority. American money, he said, should go to raising the living standards of the Arabs, not to underpinning a military effort against Israel. However, since Secretary of State Dulles was trying to negotiate a settlement of the Canal ownership and administration, Stevenson refrained from comment during August, September and early October, so as not to interfere in any way with the Administration's efforts.

Then, on October 12, during a campaign program on

nationwide television, Eisenhower made the following statement:

> I've got the best announcement that I think I can possibly make to America tonight. The progress made in the settlement of the Suez dispute this afternoon at the United Nations is most gratifying . . .
>
> It looks like there's a very great problem that's behind us.

This "announcement," it seemed to Stevenson, was inexcusable. After several days of sometimes heated discussion with his staff and with advisers in various parts of the country, he determined to speak out on the Middle Eastern question. At Cincinnati on October 19 he answered the President:

> We need to be called to labor, not lulled with rosy and misleading assurances that all is well. Leadership which fails in this is leadership to disaster.
>
> Yet a few nights ago the Republican candidate sought to make political capital out of a crisis that could engulf the world. Wars have begun over matters of far less moment than the Suez dispute—for the canal is a lifeline of the world.
>
> I have refrained until now from commenting on the Suez crisis. But the Republican candidate has introduced it, in a highly misleading way, into the campaign.
>
> A week ago he came before that so-called press conference . . . [and] announced that he had "good news" about Suez.

This is what was inexcusable, Stevenson thought, and could not be allowed to pass without challenge:

> But there is no "good news" about Suez. Why didn't the President tell us the truth? Why hasn't he told us frankly that what has happened in these past few months is that the Communist rulers of Soviet Russia have accomplished a Russian ambition that the Czars could never accom-

plish? Russian power and influence have moved into the Middle East—the oil tank of Europe and Asia and the great bridge between East and West?

His next words hung in the air with bitter sarcasm:

When the historians write of our era they may, I fear, find grim irony in the fact that when Russian power and influence were for the first time being firmly established in the Middle East, our government was loudly, proudly proclaiming our victorious conduct of the cold war and the President reported good news from Suez.

Six days later the Egyptian, Syrian, and Jordanian governments announced that they had placed their armies under a joint command. On October 29 Israel invaded Egypt. On October 30 Britain and France presented both Egypt and Israel with an ultimatum to withdraw from the canal area and lay down their arms within twelve hours. Israel agreed, but Egypt refused. On October 31 Britain and France began air attacks on Egyptian installations.

In the United Nations the United States found herself siding with the Soviet Union against her own allies in an effort to bring about a cease-fire. At almost the same moment uprisings in Hungary, stimulated at least in part by the Eisenhower-Dulles talk of "liberation," were flaring into full-scale civil war. On October 31, however, President Eisenhower expressed himself as satisfied that the Russians were making adequate concessions, and that order would soon be restored. Only hours after these words were spoken the tanks of the Red Army rumbled into Budapest to slaughter the freedom fighters in the streets; and the dying voice of the Hungarian freedom radio desperately implored America to give assistance in a struggle which, the Hungarians said, the Americans had encouraged.

The next evening, November 1, only five days from the election, Stevenson made his last ditch effort to turn the tide that was running against him:

Here we stand today. We have alienated our European allies. We have alienated Israel. We have alienated Egypt and the Arab countries. And in the UN our main associate in Middle Eastern matters now appears to be Communist Russia—in the very week when the Red Army has been shooting down the brave people of Hungary and Poland. We have lost every point in the game. I doubt if ever before in our diplomatic history has any policy been such an abysmal, such a complete and such a catastrophic failure.

He recited the record of the preceding three years, showing how one mistaken act or word of bravado had led to another until the nation's foreign policy was in a shambles. Once more he pleaded for positive steps in the Middle East, recalling his own proposal, made almost a year before, that UN patrols should be stationed on the borders between Israel and the Arab states. "I pointed out," he said, "the growing dangers in the area and suggested that United Nations guards should patrol the areas of violence and collision and keep the hostile forces apart." He left it to his hearers to imagine what a difference there would have been if the proposal had been acted upon. Forcefully he reminded the nation that he had said a year before that "it would take decisive acts of statesmanship to head-off all-out war in the Middle East." Now, in the twelfth hour both of the crisis and of the American election, he called once more for a positive policy worthy of American traditions:

The time has come to wipe the slate clean and begin anew. We must, for a change, be honest with ourselves and honest with the rest of the world. The search for peace demands the best that is in us. The time is now. We can no longer escape the challenge of history.

A majority of Americans, perhaps still wishing to escape the challenge, four days later again preferred Eisenhower to Stevenson. Public opinion students, following up the 1956 election, estimated that Eisenhower had actually gained some three million votes because fear that the United States might become involved in the Suez War led people to wish the trusted General to remain in command.

In his Chicago headquarters Stevenson knew early in the evening of election day that he would again go down to defeat. Carefully he composed a message of good wishes to the President and a personal word of farewell. Again he had no regrets, except for the disappointment of the people who had supported him. Characteristically even in defeat he uttered once again the familiar Stevensonian call for reason and progress:

> So I say to you, my dear and loyal friends, take heart —there are things more precious than political victory; there is the right to political contest. And who knows better than you who bear the fresh, painful wounds of battle.
>
> Let me add another thought for you who have traveled with me on this great journey:
>
> I have tried to chart the road to a new and better America. I want to say to all of you who have followed me that, while we have lost a battle, I am supremely confident that our cause will ultimately prevail, for America can only go forward. It cannot go backward or stand still.
>
> But even more urgent is the hope that our leaders will recognize that America wants to face up squarely to the facts of today's world . . .
>
> And, finally, the will of our society is announced by the majority. And if other nations have thought in the past few weeks that we were looking the other way and too divided to act, they will learn otherwise.

Harking back to almost his first words as a national figure in 1952, Stevenson now moved his listeners:

> What unites us is deeper than what divides us—love of freedom, love of justice, love of peace.

> May America continue under God, to be the shield
> and spear of democracy. And let us give the administra-
> tion all responsible support in the troubled times ahead.

Then, as he had done in 1952, he took his leave with that
copyrighted blend of warm sentiment and self-deprecating
humor which so endeared him to his followers:

> Now I bid you good night, with a full heart and fer-
> vent prayer that we will meet often again in the liberals'
> everlasting battle against ignorance, poverty, misery and
> war.
> Be of good cheer. And remember, my dear friends,
> what a wise man said—"A merry heart doeth good like
> a medicine, but a broken spirit dryeth the bones."
> As for me, let there be no tears. I lost an election but
> won a grandchild!

And indeed he had won a grandchild, for Adlai Ewing Stevenson IV was born to Adlai III and Nancy the previous day.

Two days before the American election, the Canadian
Minister for External Affairs, Lester Pearson, had moved in
the United Nations that as soon as a cease-fire could be negotiated a police force of United Nations troops, drawn from
several countries, be sent to patrol the borders in the Middle East. On November 6, the day after the election, Britain,
France, and Israel agreed to a cease-fire with Egypt. Within
hours the United Nations' forces took over. Adlai Stevenson
had never believed that he would win the 1956 election. But
after so rigorous, long, and exhausting a political campaign
it must have been some satisfaction to him that in the moment of his defeat his Middle Eastern policy became world
policy—not because it was his, he knew well enough, but because it was necessary. Once again, in the gravest matter
before the country and the world, Stevenson the opposition
leader, not the triumphant President, had given decisive
leadership.

II

EXHAUSTED AND ANXIOUS for privacy, during the last weeks of November Stevenson went without announcement to vacation at the plantation home of a friend in South Carolina. But reporters nevertheless soon found out his whereabouts and pestered him for an interview. There was probably only one way in which, after so many months in the headlines, he could then make news. And news he made. "I shall not again be a candidate," he said. It was stated categorically and with feeling. After his defeat in 1952 when a reporter asked whether he would run again, Stevenson had quipped, "Have that man's head examined!" But this time he left no doubt that he meant it. He spoke of the need for new, younger leaders, stressed his own weariness, adding that he would, of course, be available to assist the Democratic Party in ways other than running for President.

Upon his return to Chicago he found great bundles of mail, once more regretting his defeat, but many letters regretting even more his announcement that he would not try again. Within two years, despite his firm withdrawal, the question of a possible third nomination was again being raised by many Democratic leaders, and Gallup polls showed that he stood at the top in popular preference. Whether he might in fact have been nominated, and elected, in 1960 had he left the way open in November, 1956, no one could do better than guess. But it is certain that had he taken an equivocal, "maybe yes, maybe no" position he would not have been true either to his personal feelings or to his conception of the Presidency. In typical Stevensonian humor he told the reporters in parting, "I find that I can contemplate with complete equanimity the distinct possibility that I shall never be President of the United States!"

He was not to be President, but his defeat in 1956 was neither to remove him from the center of the American political stage nor seriously weaken his influence on matters of

policy, within his party. Shortly after the election he proposed
to his ex-running mate, Estes Kefauver, and National Chairman Paul Butler that the Democratic National Committee
establish a committee of party leaders who could speak with
some authority on behalf of the party in matters of program
and policy. He would himself remain titular leader until the
1960 convention, but he did not intend to play so active a
role as he had done between 1952 and 1956, and, in any case,
he thought that statements by the most eminent leaders acting as a group would have greater impact upon public opinion. Butler and Kefauver accepted the idea, and presently the
National Committee anounced the formation of the Democratic Advisory Council.

This unique experiment in opposition politics flourished
from its founding until it was abolished following the election
of John Kennedy in 1960. Though the Congressional leaders
were invited to join, they declined on the ground that they
would not be able to give the necessary time to the Council's
work. It was clear, however, that men like Speaker Sam Rayburn and Majority Leader Lyndon Johnson did not really
welcome the new body, seeing in it a certain rival to their own
leadership of the Democratic Party. Their analysis was correct. The Democratic Advisory Council, including such men
as Stevenson, Truman, Harriman, Kefauver, and John Kennedy, as well as potential candidates like Governor Mennen
Williams of Michigan, and Senators Hubert Humphrey of
Minnesota and Stuart Symington of Missouri, soon appeared
as a kind of "shadow cabinet," that is, the Presidential wing
of the party out of power.

The Advisory Council met regularly under the chairmanship of Butler, but the leading voice was Stevenson's.
The Council recruited panels to make studies of such spe-
cialized problems as employment, agricultural surpluses, foreign policy, military policy, and civil rights. This work was
assisted by the publication, in the Spring of 1957, of Stevenson's 1956 campaign speeches and papers, *The New Amer-*

ica.* Among the men brought into the Council's work were
the group which had served Stevenson previously under
Thomas K. Finletter's direction. Finletter himself took a leading role in raising money to support the Council and in bringing able men into its orbit. The statements of the Council
were issued over the names of the whole membership, but
the positions they defended and the attacks they launched
against the Administration's conduct typically bore the Stevensonian stamp. The work of the Council, indeed, reflected
the fact that despite his two defeats it was still the "Stevenson
era" in the Democratic Party. When the 1960 campaign got
under way, Candidate Kennedy found ready-made in the papers of the Council much of the material he needed for
speeches and statements of the alternatives the Democrats
could offer to the American people.

III

IN SEPTEMBER, 1957 the Russians, in a dramatic and startling
demonstration of the progress their scientists had been making, sent the first rocket-borne satellite into space. There
seemed also to be important military implications in the
thrust of the Sputnik's mighty engine. The Eisenhower Administration hastened to call for a stepped-up program of scientific education in American schools and colleges, and for
closer cooperation of the NATO powers in the face of the
deepening threat of Soviet Communism. Under these circumstances Secretary of State Dulles advised the President that
both the American public and the allied peoples would be
reassured by some dramatic evidence of national unity in the
United States. He suggested that Adlai Stevenson be invited
to join, at the highest level, in the preparation of American
policy for a meeting of NATO heads of state. The President
was not enthusiastic. On more than one occasion he had been
advised to seek help from Stevenson but had been unwilling

* New York: Harper and Bros., 1957.

to turn to his defeated opponent. At this juncture, however, he agreed to put aside personal feeling. Perhaps his change of mind was spurred by the launching, late in October, of a second and much larger Sputnik. At any rate Stevenson was asked to go to Washington as an adviser to the State Department. It was left undecided whether he would accompany the President to Paris for the NATO meeting.

Upon receipt of the invitation, following private conversations with Dulles, Stevenson formally consulted such Democratic leaders as Truman, Speaker Rayburn, and Senator Johnson. They unanimously advised him to accept. In a letter to President Eisenhower, Stevenson underscored the conditions upon which he agreed to serve:

> Perhaps I should take this opportunity to say what I am sure we all understand—that while I must be free to seek advice, in my informal, consultative capacity, from persons outside the Department, including leaders of my party, and also to express my views, even where they may differ from the Administration, I shall strive to promote national unity in furtherance of the great tasks before us.

In Washington Stevenson worked day and night on memoranda for Dulles' use, in conferences with State Department officials, and in extended briefings on the military and political situation. But despite the hard work he was dismayed by the atmosphere he found: "I am troubled," he wrote Dulles, "by the lack of a sense of urgency. I came to Washington to work first in 1933, and again early in 1941; both times the atmosphere was different. I wish it was now." He soon realized that regardless of his advice the Administration was determined to place military questions at the top of the NATO agenda. In Stevenson's view what was most urgently needed was closer political cooperation and a stronger sense of unity of purpose among the NATO powers. If NATO was only a military alliance inspired by the fear of Communism, it would fail in its great potential mission not only to defend but to spread the values of western civilization. To further this end Stevenson concluded that his best contribution would be to make positive suggestions for NATO activity in non-military areas. In particular, it seemed to him that since NATO included most of the wealthy nations of the world which were former colonial powers, a concerted effort by these same powers to raise the standards of living in the ex-colonial world, which was also the underdeveloped and still uncommitted world, would be the most creative program NATO could adopt. He therefore prepared several memoranda, containing broad outlines for such cooperative economic proposals, and repeatedly urged his view upon Dulles. When opportunity arose he spoke of the matter to the President. "The main threat," he wrote, for example, "is *not military aggression*, but subversion by propaganda, economic bribery and political penetration." "Have we," he asked, "any common plans to counter such ambiguous aggression?" He never received a reply. And again:

> If the Atlantic Community had multilateral economic and trade development plans it would mean a lot more to many people than its purely military anti-communism does now.

But the Administration showed little interest. Their preoccupation with military questions was so complete that even when the Italian NATO delegation made suggestions strikingly like those of Stevenson, Secretary Dulles merely indicated general agreement, with no disposition to act. Under such circumstances Stevenson declined the invitation to accompany Eisenhower to Paris. His assistance, it seemed to him, was not needed on military questions and not wanted on economic and political questions. Further, if he were to go along he would give the appearance of favoring the military emphasis which in fact he deplored. And so his uneasy and short-lived alliance with the Eisenhower Administration came to an end. The President wrote him a formal letter of thanks, but it was clear that neither side regretted the parting. Two years later, as so often happened during his years of opposition, Stevenson's view was belatedly adopted in the Administration when Under Secretary of State Dillon presided over the establishment of the Organization for Economic Cooperation and Development (OECD).

After leaving Washington Stevenson became senior partner in a distinguished New York law firm, and reduced his public activity to the minimum compatible with his position. He made fewer addresses than he had done for many years. His political activity was almost exclusively channeled through the Democratic Advisory Council. But in the summer of 1958 he found himself once more the object of national and international interest when he made an extensive tour of the Soviet Union. As he had done on his world tour of 1953, he contracted for a series of articles for *Look* magazine. With him he took two of his sons, Borden and John Fell, his law partner and assistant William Blair, and an interpreter. The tour was both extensive and intensive. Stevenson visited every major section of the Soviet Union from Leningrad to Siberia and from the Caucasus to Moscow. At many points he retraced the steps he had taken as a young man in 1926, comparing Russian progress or decline. He was entertained by factory managers, farm cooperative directors, teachers, scientists, professors, artists, politicians, and by Chairman Khrushchev himself. Everywhere he found the people friendly, "more friendly," he wrote, than they had been in 1926. But "their ignorance and anxiety about America was greater, and the industrialization more spectacular" than he had expected.

Stevenson not only studied Russian conditions as closely as he could, as he covered more than ten thousand miles, but he tried to estimate the successes and failures of Communism as a system of government and social organization. He was impressed by its material achievements. "The vast Russian land," he said, "is beginning to yield up its wealth." And the people were not discontented or fretful under the yoke of the dictatorship:

> . . . most Soviet citizens are proud and loyal, like most citizens everywhere. Nor could I detect that our negative policy toward the Soviet Union was likely to induce the Soviet collapse which has been periodically foretold from official Washington in recent years, or even contain the expansion of Soviet influence.

On the other hand, Stevenson was made more than ever aware of the dangers in any society which has no open opposition:

> But the Communist system has frailties. The imperial Czars' successors were chosen by dynastic inheritance, but in the Soviet autocracy no system of orderly transfer of power without conspiracy, violence and exile has been evolved. The present massive stability of the U.S.S.R. obscures the insidious instability of a big, modern, industrial state ruled autocratically. When a system, like the Soviet, lacks a legalized opposition, it is inherently unstable. And I suspect the reason they have not solved the problem of orderly transfer of power is that it is insoluble in the dictatorial framework.

Stevenson's *Look* articles, gathered into a best selling book, *Friends and Enemies,** were topical and descriptive for the most part. They were effectively illustrated from photographs taken by John Fell Stevenson. But the book was more than a cultivated travelogue. Stevenson's concern for western responses to the Soviet challenge grew as he came better to understand the dimensions of the Soviet achievement. Military defense against Communist aggression simply would not be a sufficient policy for the long years ahead. The arguments

---

* New York: Harper and Bros., 1959.

he had offered to Dulles and Eisenhower the year before
seemed to him now more than ever valid, even imperative:.

> . . . *the reality is the remorseless Soviet challenge which
> we have too long ignored and underestimated. They will
> use their greater flexibility to keep us off balance and on
> the defensive. They will continue to picture us as menac-
> ing and rigid to the Afro-Asian bystanders. They will
> make agreements only when it serves their purpose.
> Suspending nuclear tests with inspection is a hopeful
> possibility and would be the first break in the armaments
> deadlock. But I am less hopeful of Soviet agreement to
> larger measures of inspection of their territory because it
> would tend to convert their closed system into an open
> one and thus endanger the basis of Soviet control.*

The place to begin a positive policy was at home. Stevenson,
like an elder statesman, now admonished his readers:

> *If we can't do much with Moscow, we can do a
> lot with ourselves. The free world must set its house in
> order and keep it in order, and not just sit around, bicker-
> ing, postponing and waiting for total peace to break out.
> Moscow will be more likely to talk seriously if the West-
> ern alliance is vital and viable, the residual colonial
> problems being dealt with (while the reality of Soviet
> imperialism becomes more obvious), and above all the
> free world making a concerted effort to unite the ad-
> vanced and retarded areas in common economic enter-
> prises.*

The tone of the book was somber. Stevenson's deep faith in
democracy and in the creative spirit of the American people
was tested by the immense achievements he saw in the Soviet
Union. But that faith remained unshaken. If the will was
there the American methods of freedom would forever be
superior to those of autocracy. He told of a Polish friend who
had suggested to him that Communism was maturing and be-

coming more like democracy, while democracy would, in time, be more like Communism. This view, he thought, was unrealistic. What was hopeful was that a Polish Communist felt free to express it.

The following year Stevenson again met Khrushchev, this time on the Iowa farm of Roswell Garst. While the Russian leader was truculent and even unruly at the United Nations, his exchange with Stevenson underscored the latter's impression that Khrushchev was no Stalin-like dictator. He was, rather, a politician, conscious of dependence on his constituency, the Russian people. The more political the Russians became, Stevenson remarked, the less aggressive they would be.

IV

AT HOME after his Soviet journey Stevenson took a major part in the 1958 Congressional elections, though not to the extent he had done in 1954. He had received many requests from Congressional candidates to go into their districts and speak in their support. On a somewhat selective basis he did so, campaigning especially in California and the Northwest where the upsurge of liberalism in the Democratic Party, given its initial thrust by his 1952 campaign, continued unabated. He was swinging through California when the second crisis over Quemoy and Matsu developed. The circumstances were so strikingly like those of 1954 and the Administration's first response so belligerent that Stevenson found his earlier views as applicable then as they had been on the occasion of the first crisis.

There were two differences, however. In the intervening years the Administration had permitted, though without enthusiasm, the fortifying of the offshore islands by the Nationalist Chinese. This had inevitably provoked the Chinese Communists on the mainland without adding to the defensive strength of Formosa. The other difference was that during the same period Stevenson's views on Quemoy and Matsu had come to prevail in the United States. Thus in 1958 he did not have the problem of rallying public opinion. No sooner had the Administration begun to suggest, off the record, that the United States might go to the defense of the islands, than Senator Theodore Green, Chairman of the Senate Foreign Relations Committee, wrote a letter to the President warning him that there was no popular or Congressional support for a military adventure over Quemoy and Matsu. Green counselled a cautious policy which would restrain the Nationalist Chinese from action that might embroil the United States. The President's reply was a caustic reminder that it is the President who is responsible for foreign policy. But he nevertheless reassured Senator Green and the public that no precipitate action would be taken. It was again apparent that Secretary Dulles and Admiral Radford favored an aggressive policy, but none was adopted. Strong talk was replaced by a mission of Secretary of Defense McElroy to Formosa to persuade the Nationalists to reduce their garrisons on the islands and thus reduce the tension. Presently the crisis died out. Stevenson himself was content to remind his audiences of what he had said in 1955 on the same issue, while giving his enthusiastic backing to Senator Green.

After the 1958 election, again won with a great margin by the Democrats, Stevenson withdrew almost entirely from public affairs. He spoke occasionally at universities (he was the recipient of honorary degrees from dozens of universities both in the United States and abroad) or before conferences on international affairs but avoided political meetings. In January, 1959 he gave the first annual lecture, in Washington's Constitution Hall, in memory of the eminent liberal clergyman A. Powell Davies. This address, one of Stevenson's finest, dealt with the moral crisis in the United States.* In a striking

---

* Because it displays the quality of Stevenson's mind better, perhaps, than any of his other addresses or writings, the text of this lecture is given in an appendix, pp. 201-215.

figure, "America's broken mainspring," he spoke of the discrepancy between the technological achievements of the United States and its flaccid body politic. It was like a fine watch whose mainspring is slack. Stevenson asked why this should be so. If the spring was broken no repair would be possible; but if the watch only needed to be wound there was yet time. Senator Stuart Udall had spoken of Stevenson, in a *New Republic* article, as the "conscience of the country." The Davies Lecture was a splendid articulation of that conscience. *Life* magazine, which had for years defended Eisenhower against Stevenson's criticisms, seemed to change its mind at last. In a full page editorial entitled "The Cost of Easy Options" *Life* called the lecture "the best recent statement of this informed worry," and quoted from it extensively.

Throughout 1959, despite his infrequent appearances, Stevenson figured significantly in speculation regarding the 1960 presidential nomination. Many leading citizens, speaking as individuals, advised the Democrats to nominate Stevenson again. Among these were Mrs. Roosevelt, former Senator Herbert Lehman of New York, Mrs. Agnes Meyer, owner of the *Washington Post*, Barry Bingham of the Louisville *Courier Journal* and Walter Lippmann. The polls continued to show that Stevenson was the favorite potential candidate among the rank and file of the Democratic voters. They also showed that he could defeat Vice President Nixon in the election. On the other hand partisans of Senator Kennedy, the most active probable candidate, argued that Stevenson could not win because he would be tagged as a two-time loser. Kennedy himself was quietly attempting to persuade leading Stevenson workers of other years to join his cause as the best way to realize the Stevensonian ideas to which they were committed. Some, like John Kenneth Galbraith, became members of Kennedy's organization.

Under these circumstances, efforts were made by some influential leaders of the Democratic Party to persuade Stevenson to change his mind. Privately, some of his close friends

argued that while his 1956 statement had precluded his giving
encouragement to his supporters to work on his behalf, it only
committed him to making no active campaign for the nomination. Stevenson's response was consistent and emphatic. He
had meant what he said. He was not and would not be a candidate, and would not give encouragement to people who
wished to advance his name. The time had come, he said, for
other and younger men "eager for the fray" to take over. He
would stay out. He would endorse no one, so that the race
could be wide open. When Senator Humphrey announced
his candidacy, taking Stevenson at his word, the party's two
leading prospects were both Stevensonians. Thus while he
watched other men vie for the honor he had twice been given,
Stevenson could take satisfaction in hearing the ideas he had
stood for over the years advocated earnestly and effectively
by a new generation of Democratic leaders.

But his efforts to keep himself out of the nomination
speculation were unavailing. By the winter of 1959-1960 he
had to recognize that his stature, simply as a private citizen,
was so great that it was impossible not to think of him as a
presidential possibility. When, for example, the active candidates approached Governor David Lawrence of Pennsylvania
for an endorsement, that veteran Democratic leader took a
position of neutrality, quickly adding that in his opinion
"Governor Stevenson is by far the best qualified man in the
country." Partly to get away from politics altogether while
Kennedy and Humphrey were battling in the primaries, and
partly to "continue his education," Stevenson decided to make
a long and thorough tour of Latin America during the early
months of 1960. He hoped, he said, to return from this trip
"a much better citizen of the hemisphere."

In the course of his journey he must have felt at times
as though he were not merely a citizen of the hemisphere,
but the first citizen. Perhaps no other American had ever been
received in Latin America with such enthusiasm. Two years
earlier Vice President Nixon had gone to Latin America on

a "good will" tour only to be hissed and stoned and even spat upon in such cities as Caracas and Lima, and treated everywhere as a symbol of distrust of the United States. Stevenson, though a private citizen, effectively reversed the current of feeling. In each of the capitals he was received by the head of government and shown the most cordial friendship not only by officials but also by crowds of plain people who came to see him and to display their feeling that he was the authentic representative of that "Good Neighbor" policy identified in Latin America with the Democratic Party since the time of Franklin Roosevelt.

One description of a Stevenson reception, by Ralph McGill in the Atlanta *Constitution,* may serve to suggest the quality of Stevenson's whole tour:

> Stevenson arrived at Bogota. He and his group were whisked, so to speak, from airport to bullring. A massed group outside, which was in a near state of rebellion because it could not obtain tickets, let up a great cry of acclaim. Inside, the massed benches let loose such a roar on Stevenson's entry that he flinched, thinking nothing less than a riot had erupted. His admiring hosts, the president and officials, assured him that it was his welcome.
>
> Speeches were made. The great gates of the arena opened for the ritual of the bullfight processional. It brought further salutes to the visiting American.
>
> Nor was this the end. The matadors dedicated their bulls to him. And when the long hours of death in the afternoon were done, Stevenson was hoisted to the shoulders of the crowd, along with the three matadors, and carried about the ring to the vast delight of the multitude which kept up a Niagara of shouts. Chief among them was "uno," meaning the first or the best.

At that moment, McGill concluded, "the life of a topflight matador seemed to Stevenson much more enjoyable and happy than that of a presidential candidate."

But beneath the surface of ceremony and personal popularity, hard work was going on, as on Stevenson's previous tours. He had taken with him a leading expert on Latin America, Carleton Sprague Smith, William Benton, a former Assistant Secretary of State, and Blair, his friend and assistant. Intensive studies were made of political, economic, and social conditions. As he had done on his world tour back in 1953, Stevenson insisted on learning the views of opposition leaders everywhere, whether these men were allowed to act in the open or had been forced underground. Stevenson was convinced that the Eisenhower Administration, by dealing only with leaders actually in power, however precarious their hold, was failing to understand the true quality of the revolutionary changes going on in Latin America. He intended to avoid making this mistake. And so he did what he could to cultivate and understand what Harlan Cleveland aptly called "next governments."

What Stevenson learned disturbed him deeply. Castro-type revolutions, he concluded, were bound to occur in other Latin American countries unless drastic land reforms were put into effect, unless the abysmal gap between the few rich and the many poor was rapidly narrowed, and unless the United States displayed beyond question its concern for the welfare of plain people in Latin America by supporting change instead of blocking it through assistance to reactionary military and business leaders. Writing again in *Look* magazine, Stevenson acidly commented:

> I was in Latin America last spring at the same time as President Eisenhower. I traveled through twelve countries in eight weeks. The President went to four countries in ten days. He came back optimistic. I came back deeply concerned.

But a year later he had reason to be more hopeful. The Kennedy Administration, following Stevenson's principal suggestions, established the Alliance for Progress, based on the principle that American financial assistance to raise living standards in Latin America would be tied to firm guarantees of reform by the Latin American governments. Stevenson himself was to return to Latin America on an urgent mission, this time official, to shore up American relations after the disaster at the Bay of Pigs.

V

THAT ADLAI STEVENSON DID in the end become a kind of candidate for the 1960 Democratic nomination was owing to events quite beyond his control. Only if he had stayed entirely away from the country until after the Democratic Convention would he have been able to escape "unscathed," as he put it. Upon his return from Latin America he found a noisy crowd at the airport and an overflowing press conference. He wanted to talk about his trip; the newsmen wanted to talk about the nomination. Would he bcome a candidate? Would he enter any primaries, Oregon, for example? Would he accept the nomination if it were offered? What about the talk of a draft? Patiently Stevenson answered all such leading questions in the negative, except the question whether he would respond to a draft. To this he gave an answer which was frequently repeated during the remaining weeks before the convention: he would not talk about the subject at all, since if he said he would accept a draft he would be said to be seeking a draft, while if he said he would not accept a draft he would be called a "draft evader." This formulation gave scant comfort to his friends who were hoping for some positive word. But it sent emissaries of Humphrey and Kennedy hurrying to ask for his support of their candidate.

The next day, in a Jefferson Day speech at Charlottesville, Virginia, he struck out at the Eisenhower Administration for lack of leadership and failure of ideas. The language was strong, like that of a candidate. The reception accorded him was full of the excitement characteristic of his presidential campaigns. The press treated his remarks and his manner as though he were a candidate. Matters, he concluded, had gone too far. He would simply have to refuse to make public appearances, except for a few to which he had long committed himself.

Stevenson's voluntary withdrawal from political activity was closely followed by Senator Kennedy's decisive victory over Humphrey in the West Virginia primary on May 10. When the results of that contest were announced it appeared that Kennedy was an almost certain choice for the Democratic nomination. Stevenson was advised by some of his close friends to endorse Kennedy, thereby bringing an end to the pre-convention maneuvering, and incidentally, putting himself in a strong position to be named Secretary of State should Kennedy be elected. There could have been no doubt that Stevenson would be interested in heading the State Department under a Democratic President. But he was certainly not willing to involve himself in anyone's candidacy for such a purpose. In any case his respect for Senator Kennedy's qualifications to be President was no greater than for some of the other available men. He had promised all the candidates that he would remain neutral. And so he did.

Then, in stunning succession, came the announcement that American U-2 flyer Powers had been shot down and arrested over the Soviet Union, that Secretary of Defense McElroy had ordered a worldwide alert of American combat forces, that President Eisenhower had ignored all diplomatic precedent, and perhaps wisdom as well, by taking personal responsibility for Powers' illegal flight, and, finally, on May 16, the news that Chairman Khrushchev had broken off the Summit Conference then being held in Paris. At the moment this last news became known, Stevenson was testifying in Washington before a Senate Committee on his proposal that the Federal Communications Commission be permitted to waive their rules so that the television networks could give free time for a series of debates between the presidential candidates during the forthcoming election. When the news was brought into the hearing room, the proceedings were adjourned and Stevenson immediately became the center of attention from newsmen demanding comment. At the moment he merely observed that "this is terribly sad news." Later in the day he joined with his colleagues in the Democratic Party's official leadership, Speaker Rayburn and Majority Leader Johnson, in a cable to Khrushchev urging him to reconsider. Stevenson's proposal before the Senate, forgotten at the moment of crisis, was later adopted and led to the "Great Debate" in the fall of 1960 between Nixon and Kennedy and thus, in the opinion of many observers, to the election of Kennedy.

The dramatic and discouraging news from Europe had a special significance for Stevenson. Overnight the question of the Democratic nomination seemed once again far from settled. From many sections of the country came a new call for Stevenson to become a candidate. A National Draft Stevenson Committee which had been sputtering for some months gained new importance. A committee of eminent citizens placed a full page advertisement in the New York Times and other newspapers urging Stevenson's nomination. Among the signers were Mrs. Eleanor Roosevelt, Herbert Lehman, Senators Mike Monroney and John Carroll, Mrs. Marshall Field, Thomas K. Finletter, and Mrs. Eugene Meyer. Monroney and James Doyle, a Democratic leader from Wisconsin, established a formal Stevenson headquarters in Washington and began to solicit delegates. It was late, too late as it turned out, but the enthusiasm coming up from the "grass roots" of American life was felt throughout the nation. Millions of signatures were gathered on petitions to be presented at the Democratic Convention. "Stevenson Caravans" were organized to drive across the country to Los Angeles, where the convention was to be held in mid-June. Stevenson buttons and pennants and automobile stickers began to appear everywhere.

Stevenson himself, though he would not alter his position as a non-candidate, felt a responsibility to speak out on the great issue of foreign policy, and did so in another memorable speech. At the Cook County Democratic Dinner on May 19 he lashed out at the failures of the Administration. He blamed the break-up of the Summit Conference directly upon Khrushchev. But, in unforgettable language, he placed a heavy burden of responsibility upon the President and his associates:

> . . . we handed Khrushchev the crowbar and the sledge-hammer to wreck the meeting. Without our series of blunders Mr. Khrushchev would not have had a pretext for making his impossible demand and wild charges. Let there be no mistake about that . . .

He recited a record of mistakes unhappily reminiscent of the record he had read four years before in the midst of the Suez crisis. Yet so great was the continuing personal prestige of the President that once again the popular response was to rally to his support rather than hold him to account. Leading newspapers welcomed Stevenson's forthright statement of the issue. Yet among the leading public men in both parties only Senator Kennedy followed Stevenson's lead and forthrightly assigned responsibility to the President. But thereafter the issue was drawn. If Stevenson was not to be the candidate against Nixon, at least the people would know what the alternatives were.

At the Los Angeles convention Stevenson's conduct was somewhat ambiguous. He continued to speak of himself as a non-candidate; he made no effort to attract delegates. Yet he did not ask the leaders of the Draft Stevenson Movement to stop their activities. And on a nationwide television program he said that his supporters had "made him a candidate." His reception at the Los Angeles airport dwarfed those of other Democratic leaders. Around the Sports Arena huge crowds gathered whenever he appeared. The galleries were filled with Stevenson rooters.

On the second night of the convention occurred an incident filled with drama which might have altered the course of American political history. Stevenson had decided that he would go to the floor of the convention to underline the fact that he was a delegate, not a candidate. His arrival was the signal for one of the most vociferous and prolonged demonstrations ever known at a presidential nominating convention. At first it was confined mainly to the galleries. But as it continued, delegates began to join in from the floor. In the end the Chairman, Governor Collins of Florida, had to invite Stevenson to the rostrum in order to restore order. Seasoned professional politicians watching the scene agreed afterward that if Stevenson had grasped the opportunity thus afforded him to make a forceful "Stevensonian" speech, he might well have stampeded the convention into nominating him. While a majority of the delegates certainly favored Kennedy, their devotion to their man was lacking in the sort of enthusiasm Stevenson had always been able to stir up. Many, in fact, were for Kennedy only because they believed Stevenson to be unavailable. If, at this fateful moment, he had made clear his desire for the nomination, even without any explicit statement to that effect, it appeared that a realignment of forces would quickly take place.

But such self-serving would have been wholly out of character. There was no doubt that Stevenson would have accepted the nomination, even welcomed it. "If they want me to lead them, I shall lead them," he had said a day earlier. But he would not act to get that nomination. On the rostrum, when quiet at last prevailed, he merely waved and then made some characteristically self-deprecating remarks. The great crowd laughed and cheered, but the potency of the moment had been dissipated. Thereafter there was no real doubt that Kennedy would be nominated. And so he was, on the first ballot. Senator Eugene McCarthy of Minnesota made a stirring speech when he placed Stevenson's name in nomination, and Hubert Humphrey announced that he wished his delegates to vote for Stevenson. But since so many were pledged to Kennedy at the start, the Stevenson strength was necessarily unavailable until after the first or even the second ballot. And that reserve was never tested, since Kennedy's first ballot strength held.

Thus the leadership of the Democratic Party passed to the younger man, as Stevenson had foretold. But in defeat the Stevensonians were filled with pride. It was their man who had electrified the convention. It was their man's ideas which were written into the party platform and into the acceptance speech of the candidate. And the candidate himself had matured under Stevenson's influence. Even the Republicans had written Stevensonian ideas into their platform, calling as they did for an end to nuclear testing and for a pooling of NATO resources for economic assistance to the underdeveloped countries of the former colonial world.

Adlai Stevenson's career as a politician reached its poignant closing moment at Los Angeles the day after John Kennedy's nomination, when he met with his die-hard supporters to say farewell. There were few dry eyes as Stevenson addressed them in words of warm gratitude. And he sent them away certain in their hearts that their "lost cause" was nevertheless the right cause:

> You have given me something far more precious than the nomination; you have taught me a lesson I should have learned long ago—to take counsel always of your courage and never of your fears.

But if Adlai Stevenson as a politician was now, after some campaign speeches on behalf of Kennedy, to make his exit from the stage of political affairs, there was general agreement throughout the nation that he must be given some new and different opportunity to use his great gifts on behalf of the nation.

8

Diplomat on the World Stage

I

NO SOONER HAD John F. Kennedy won his narrow victory over Richard Nixon than buttons and stickers began to appear in many cities reading "Stevenson for Secretary of State." The devoted Stevensonians had another campaign under way. And it was unique. There was no precedent for a public campaign to persuade a President to name a favorite political figure as his Secretary of State. In 1913 President Wilson, to his later regret, had named William Jennings Bryan to that highest appointive office. But Wilson was aknowledging in the Bryan appointment his debt for the presidential nomination itself. Kennedy, on the contrary, had no political obligation to Adlai Stevenson. Indeed, it was Stevenson who had provided the only serious obstacle to Kennedy's nomination. At the convention and afterwards some of Kennedy's close advisers were heard to say emphatically that after his failure to support Kennedy at Los Angeles, Stevenson would never be Secretary of State. The drive to influence the President-elect therefore had political overtones. It was intended to show that Stevenson still had an important political following of which Kennedy would need to take account in forming his administration and formulating his policy.

To Stevenson the movement was both a compliment and an embarrassment. He knew that he was well qualified to be Secretary of State and, under some circumstances, would no doubt have been pleased to have the appointment. But as a matter of principle he thought that a President should have a completely free hand in the selection of his Cabinet. And he was fully aware of the political objections raised by his lack of enthusiasm for Kennedy before and during the convention. He had campaigned strenuously for Kennedy's election, but was under no illusion that he had thereby obligated the President-elect to make him Secretary of State.

Soon the newspapers were speculating that Stevenson would be offered the post as U.S. delegate to the United Nations. The idea was that the former Democratic leader would lend prestige and dignity to that office while, at the same time, he was effectively shunted out of the center of governmental policy-making. Stevenson's reaction to these stories was that if they were true he would stay in private life. Some of his close friends advised him to do so in any case. Stevenson, they said, was more useful to the country as an independent voice on foreign policy than he could be under the discipline of responsibility to the Administration. For several weeks the matter of his future status remained in doubt. When President-elect Kennedy did at last call upon Stevenson, however, all prior speculation turned out to be mistaken.

Kennedy did indeed ask Stevenson to become U.S. Representative to the United Nations. But he proposed also that Stevenson become a full member of the Cabinet and that he participate in all aspects of foreign policy planning. This would include sitting in the National Security Council where matters of national defense would be considered. He would have freedom to nominate his own staff of colleagues and subordinates, including recommending the Assistant Secretary of State for International Organization Affairs whose job was to "backstop" the United Nations Mission from Washington. The President-elect assured Stevenson that he wished him to play a central part in the Administration, that he would have direct access to the President at all times, and that his appointment would underscore a new American emphasis upon the importance of the United Nations. If Stevenson was disappointed at not receiving the appointment as Secretary of State he gave no sign. The alternative proposed by Kennedy was attractive. Stevenson was prepared to accept it, provided only that the Secretary of State would be a man congenial to his views of foreign policy and the United Nations. When Kennedy announced the appointment of Dean Rusk, then President of the Rockefeller Foundation and a former Assistant Secretary of State, Stevenson was pleased and hastened to accept his own appointment.

Before the Senate Foreign Relations Committee, and a packed gallery, on January 18, Stevenson answered questions as to his qualifications to represent the United States at the United Nations, and gave a full statement of his views. "I welcome this opportunity," he said, "to serve the United States in the United Nations. I do not minimize its difficulties, but I also regard it as a great opportunity." He recalled that he had played a part in the founding of the UN and served in the first American delegations. Since that time the membership had more than doubled, and UN operations were going on throughout the world. The United States, Stevenson said, believed that "the United Nations is man's best hope for peace. But it is something more than that. It is our best hope for fashioning a peace marked with freedom and justice." He called attention to the fact that while the Communist nations were included in the UN, the organization itself was "an extension of Western ideas." This, he said, was "why Khrushchev pounds the desk in frustration."

It was a fair measure of the respect in which Adlai Stevenson was held that no Senator asked him an unfriendly question. All, on the contrary, Republican and Democrat alike, complimented him on his performance and wished him well in his new role. Their vote to approve his appointment was unanimous.

At John Kennedy's inauguration Adlai Stevenson sat beside Dean Rusk on the platform. The next day when the Cabinet was sworn into office by the new President, Stevenson, at the insistence of Rusk and his colleagues, headed the list. At the first meeting of the Cabinet it was Stevenson, again at the request of his colleagues, who made the formal response on behalf of the Cabinet to the President's opening remarks. His high position in the Administration thus underscored by these ceremonial events, the new U.S. Representative took up his residence in New York.

At the United Nations Stevenson presented his credentials to the President of the Security Council, to the President of the General Assembly, and to his old friend Secretary General Dag Hammarskjöld. He found many friends from early UN days still there. His colleagues from other nations welcomed him with warmth and enthusiasm such as had not previously been accorded to any other delegate. Partly this was because many already knew and liked him personally, but partly, too, it was because they saw in the appointment of one of the most distinguished living Americans a sign that the new Administration was sincere in its announced policy of greater emphasis upon worldwide cooperation through the United Nations. If Adlai Stevenson were coming to the UN, the UN was being "promoted" in the priorities of United States policy, so some veteran UN officials and diplomats put it.

But the "honeymoon" did not last long. When Stevenson arrived, the UN was struggling with the problem of the

Katangese rebellion in the Congo. The United States had fully supported the recommendations of the Secretary General and voted for the UN police force which was then striving to unite the huge former Belgian colony under a central government chosen by and responsible to the people. The UN's official position was under attack from the right by those who saw in President Tshombe of Katanga a valiant foe of Communism and a friend of the business interests of the West. From the left the Soviet Union and the Communist bloc argued that the central government was no better than a front for Western "colonialism." In the Security Council Stevenson found himself immediately pitted, for the first of many bouts, against Valerian Zorin, the tough Soviet delegate who had previously distinguished himself by directing the suppression of the Hungarian freedom fighters in 1956. From the first Stevenson sought to conduct the debates at the level of a dignified exchange of opinions. He refused to be ruffled by Zorin's name-calling propaganda, while patiently explaining the American view. He was "scoring" well in the contest, in the eyes both of his UN fellow delegates and of the world press, when the tragic fiasco at the Bay of Pigs in Cuba nearly rendered his position at the UN untenable.

In April, 1961, acting upon the advice of both his intelligence officials and the Joint Chiefs of Staff, President Kennedy gave his approval to a secret plan for the invasion of Cuba by an army of Cuban exiles assisted by American agents of the Central Intelligence Agency (CIA) and financed by American money. No American troops or planes were involved. The plan had been initiated many months before by the Eisenhower Administration, and the new President apparently felt that he was to some degree obligated to honor commitments made by his predecessor. Among his close advisers in the White House Kennedy also found strong support for the venture. For reasons which were never revealed, Stevenson was neither consulted nor informed in advance of the decision to permit the invasion of Cuba. Had he known of the plan he would certainly have opposed it vigorously as an unwarranted act of aggression which would do incalculable damage to the standing of the United States with other Latin American nations. This may have been one reason for keeping him uninformed. Another may have been the somewhat cynical notion that he could defend the position of the United States in the United Nations more successfully if he did not know the extent of U.S. involvement.

The exile invading force, lacking air cover, swiftly met with disaster at the Bay of Pigs. But while the action was going on Zorin promptly charged the United States with aggression, as, of course, did the Cuban delegate. In the Security Council, relying on materials sent to him by the State Department, Stevenson asserted emphatically that the United States had no part in the affair. He even showed pictures of bombing planes over Cuban targets which, he said, were operated by Cuban pilots defecting from the Cuban air force. Angry exchanges took place. Stevenson's integrity was questioned. But he stood his ground. Then, in the wake of the total defeat of the expedition and the capture by Castro's forces of more than a thousand prisoners, President Kennedy publicly accepted responsibility for the whole affair. Stevenson had, in effect, been duped by his own government.

At this juncture Adlai Stevenson had to make a difficult decision. To continue at his post, with his effectiveness perhaps seriously impaired, was a personally painful prospect. Yet to resign at such a moment of tension and danger would be, in his view, unpatriotic, since he would be putting his own peace of mind ahead of the needs of his country. He elected to place the matter directly before the President, agreeing to remain if his position in the Administration were satisfactorily clarified. The President was evidently regretful. He assured Stevenson that no important foreign policy decisions would thereafter be made without his participation, and emphasized his desire that Stevenson remain at the United

Nations. In the years following more than one attempt was made to suggest that the relations between the President and his Representative to the United Nations were strained and near to breaking. But such rumors were without foundation. With Assistant Secretary of State Harlan Cleveland in Washington serving as channel for communication of routine business, and the telephone keeping him in direct touch with the President and Secretary of State Rusk on matters of high policy, Stevenson often told friends that he could not ask for better relations with the leaders of the Administration. In addition he made frequent trips to Washington for conferences and to attend meetings of the Cabinet and National Security Council.

II

AFTER THE GENERAL ASSEMBLY had adjourned in the spring of 1961, President Kennedy asked Stevenson to undertake a vitally important mission to Latin America. The ostensible purpose of the tour was to prepare the way for negotiation of agreements between the United States and the various Latin American governments under the new Alliance for Progress. But behind this important objective lay the President's realization that Latin American misgivings after the Bay of Pigs were more likely to be overcome by reassurances from Adlai Stevenson than by the words of any other American. The prestige of Fidel Castro throughout Latin America was at that time at its highest point. No matter what his relations with the Soviet Union and China might be, no matter that his regime was daily more and more openly Communist, what was most impressive to many Latin Americans was the simple fact that Castro and his Cuban militia had repulsed and routed an invasion backed and financed by the United States. Old cries of "Yankee imperialism" were everywhere being revived; *Fidelismo* was boasting that it could lead the way to a new independence from the United States.

Wiser heads in the governments of such nations as Brazil and Argentina, Colombia and Venezuela were not deluded, but so numerous were the Fidelistas that no politician could safely ignore them. Only the almost legendary figure of Stevenson might, perhaps, effectively counter this political current. But there was no certainty that even he, acting not as the beloved private citizen and friend of Latin America but as an American emissary, would not be rejected by Latin American opinion.

Setting out in June, with a small staff of State Department officials, Stevenson traveled 18,000 miles through ten countries. The initial response to his arrival in each capital was less warmly enthusiastic than it had been in 1960. But there were no demonstrations against him or his party and no untoward incidents took place, such as had marred other American missions. The crowds were immense. As he spoke informally to them, people seemed to remember that this was after all the same Stevenson whose understanding and sympathy for their problems had touched them in the past. In him they found an authentic spokesman of the American spirit. At each stop initial reserve gave way to warm enthusiasm. The cry was "Viva Kennedy! Viva Stevenson!" There was no lingering doubt that the journey was a great popular success.

In the formal and informal conversations Stevenson held with heads of government and foreign ministers there was much candid talk. The American made no secret of his government's regret for the Bay of Pigs incident, at the same time reminding his Latin American friends that the United States had no use for Communism and would not stand idly by while the Soviet Union penetrated the hemisphere. The way to frustrate Communism, Stevenson said, was through the concerted action of all the governments and peoples of the Americas. This meant not only, or even primarily, sanctions against Castro's regime in Cuba, but fundamental reforms everywhere—the sort of reform that would give the workers and peasants, especially the masses of people on the land, the sense of belonging, the conviction that a great revolution to raise their standard of living was being carried on with United States encouragement and direct assistance. The way, in short, to defeat Communism was to rid these lands of the conditions which breed Communism—to make freedom and democracy work. The Alliance for Progress, Stevenson emphasized, must be based on agreement to such reforms by all concerned, and to the investment of capital funds in projects and programs directly beneficial to the people. No longer could the military be permitted to eat up dollars in unnecessary armaments; no longer could corrupt governments be permitted to syphon off aid funds for the benefit of the rich and privileged.

Stevenson was under no illusion about the difficulties of his mission. The prospect of great sums of United States money would bring at least some cynical assurances of cooperation, especially from the military classes. At the same time, masses of people were deeply stirred by the symbol of Fidel Castro, and many thoughtful people, as Stevenson had foretold years before, were recalling McCarthyism and accusing the United States of once more indulging in irresponsible red-baiting. But publicizing the principles of the Alliance for Progress would make cheating more difficult, and help allay the fears of the people. And, in Stevenson's view, the newer leaders in many countries were sincere and patriotic men who fully appreciated the need for democratic revolution. The time had come, he thought, when real progress could be made. Over and over again he underlined his own and President Kennedy's view that American aid was not to be given as a weapon against Communism, but, as the President had said in his Inaugural Address, "because it is right."

Upon his return Stevenson wrote a long report for Secretary Rusk and the President, portions of which were made public in an article in the *New York Times Sunday Magazine*. He outlined the Latin American problem in these terms:

. . . seldom have democracy and governmental stability been subjected in South America to more severe strain and attack than at the present time. The Communist forces, emboldened by Castro's example in Cuba, have increased their aggressiveness. Rightwing groups jealous of ancient privileges are, in many areas, a menace to liberal representative regimes. An unholy community of interest joins the two extremes of Left and Right: the overthrow of the working democracy that could frustrate the revolutionary aims of the one and abolish the power of the other to perpetuate social injustices.

The accuracy of Stevenson's analysis was unhappily borne out by a continuing series of rebellions and disturbances in many countries of Latin America.

The only way to counteract this dangerous and ambiguous threat to freedom, Stevenson urged, was to give democracy "meaning."

. . . recognition of the threat from Cuba, translated only into political or economic action against its Government, might well increase rather than eliminate the Communist threat by investing Fidelismo with an aura of martyrdom. Such recognition must, most importantly, be translated into acts on the home front to eliminate the attraction of Castro-Communism for ordinary people who want action—as opposed to fine words—on problems they feel in their flesh and bones.

In the following November President Kennedy asked Stevenson to follow up his Latin American tour with a special mission to confer with President Frondizi of Argentina on questions facing the Alliance for Progress. The Argentine President had, in fact, suggested that he would appreciate the appointment of Stevenson to represent the United States in conversations which were to be held in Trinidad. Again taking with him a small staff of State Department experts on Latin America, Stevenson met Frondizi on November 26 and 27. The liberal American and the liberal

Argentinian understood one another well. Frondizi's purpose
was to obtain reassurance that the United States was not
simply once again tying a foreign aid program to anti-Com-
munism, but had in mind, rather, the long range improvement of life in the Latin American states. Stevenson, for his
part, as representative of the United States, was hopeful that
Frondizi might become a symbol of a new liberalism in Latin
America to offset both the Castroist agitators and the right
wing exploiters of Latin American workers and peasants.
Though the talks were highly successful, they proved abortive
when, a few months later, Frondizi was overthrown by a
coup d'etat which returned Argentina to the hands of the
reactionaries.

III

BETWEEN MISSIONS to Latin America, in the summer of 1961,
Stevenson went to Europe to attend meetings of United
Nations organizations in Geneva. At the President's request
he talked privately with heads of state and foreign ministers
on such matters as the tension over Berlin and the quarrel
between France and Tunis. His mediation was given a measure
of credit by President Bourguiba of Tunis when the latter
dispute was resolved.

Back at New York the United Nations was shocked and
thrown into a state of dangerous uncertainty when, on September 18, Secretary General Hammarskjöld was killed in an
airplane accident in the Congo. For years Hammarskjöld had
patiently threaded his way through the tensions between
East and West, always building the prestige and authority
of the United Nations as the only real alternative to chaos
and war. In his hands the Secretariat of the United Nations
had become an executive branch of the world organization.
From unarmed observers in the Middle East, to battle-ready
troops along the borders of Israel, to the United Nations army
striving to maintain the peace and establish the integrity of

the Congo, Hammarskjöld had presided over the growth of the United Nations as an active force for peace. Under his administration, too, were the many growing welfare and development activities of the United Nations. So much real power had he come to wield, on the side of peace and freedom, that the Communist bloc, headed by the Soviet Union, saw in him an arch-enemy of their purposes. For some time the Russians had been stating that they would not support his re-election in 1963 and that the Secretary General's office must be divided into three—the so-called "troika." Under this plan there would be three officials, one from the West, one from the Communist bloc, and one neutral who must all agree before action could be taken. Now, while the world was in mourning, the Russians served notice that they would press this troika plan instead of agreeing to a successor to Hammarskjöld.

Stevenson, who was saddened by the loss of a close personal friend, now found himself leading the forces who wished to preserve Hammarskjöld's conception of the Secretary Generalship in the choice of his successor. While set speeches in the Security Council could help to dramatize the problem before the world, Stevenson knew that the decision would have to be reached by quiet, off-stage diplomacy. First he met several times with Zorin privately in order to assess the degree of importance the Russians in fact attached to their stand. He concluded that Zorin had been instructed to make an all-out effort to break up the Secretariat.

The best defense, clearly, was to rally those nations of the Afro-Asian "uncommitted" bloc who were receiving the most benefits from the United Nations and thus could most readily appreciate the advantage to themselves of a strong UN executive not subject to veto by either East or West. These were the same nations, of course, which it was continuing Russian policy to woo. Increasingly they had been siding with the Communist bloc in UN voting. As Stevenson talked with the delegates from these nations he earnestly emphasized the evident fact that the troika plan would cripple the United Nations as an active agency in world affairs, leaving it little more than a debating society. This, said Stevenson, was precisely the Communist intention. Russian fears of the United Nations as an instrument of freedom were, he said, justified. Thus it was to the vital interest of the newly independent and still weak nations of Africa and Asia to keep the UN'strong. This was the surest way, he argued, for them to avoid being squeezed between the great powers. Some showed fear of Soviet reprisals if they should vote against the troika. But Stevenson countered by showing how much more they would be at the mercy of the Soviet Union if they allowed the UN to be so tragically weakened. In the end he rounded up enough votes to secure the election of U Thant of Burma to fill the unexpired term of Hammarskjöld. At any rate he allowed Zorin to suppose that he had the votes. The Russian, seeing a major defeat for Soviet policy and influence approaching, reversed his position and asked Stevenson if the Soviet Union could join in the recommendation of Thant's election. Thant was unanimously elected. It was a resounding diplomatic triumph for the United States and for Stevenson personally. A year and a half later, despite Soviet threats to revive the troika plan, Thant was elected to a full term, thus preserving for the next period the integrity and executive strength of the United Nations.

Coincident with his success at the United Nations, Stevenson was flattered by requests from Democratic leaders in Illinois that he accept the nomination for the United States Senate to run in the 1962 election against Senate Minority Leader Everett Dirksen. For a moment Stevenson appears to have been tempted. He felt deep obligations to the Democrats of Illinois who had given him first chance at a public career many years before. And his partisan feelings were stirred at the prospect of meeting an old political enemy face to face. Dirksen, a favorite of the *Chicago Tribune*, had been a vituperative critic of Stevenson ever since his days as Governor of Illinois. The possibility of retiring Senator Dirksen from public life was an inviting prospect! On the other hand, Stevenson had little desire to re-enter the political wars, and his post at the United Nations was deeply satisfying. He consulted with President Kennedy, allowing it to be known that the matter was under discussion. The President, for political reasons, would have been happy to have so strong a candidate run against Dirksen. But for more compelling reasons of national interest he thought Stevenson was more valuable in the United Nations. If Stevenson should decide to run for the Senate, however, the President would be glad to go out to Illinois and campaign for him. In a few days Stevenson concluded that he would remain at the UN. But this brief political flurry no doubt strengthened his position in the Administration by reminding the President and the White House staff that Stevenson still had an important independent political ·following.

IV

ADLAI STEVENSON's most dramatic action in the United Nations came in October, 1962 during the crisis over Russian bases in Cuba. When President Kennedy became convinced by American intelligence reports that the Russians were building nuclear missile bases in Cuba and sending planes capable of carrying nuclear bombs, he was faced with perhaps the most serious challenge to the security of the United States since World War II. That he must take some drastic action was certain. What it should be required the most careful and searching consideration. Stevenson played a major part in formulating the recommendation which the President accepted. Some advisers were prepared to recommend direct military action, either by air strike or invasion. Others preferred a blockade of Cuba accompanied by a demand that the Russians dismantle the bases and remove the bombers.

Stevenson agreed with those who favored strong action to secure the removal of the offensive weapons. But he wished also, if the first steps were successful, to make use of the occasion for negotiations with the Soviet Union looking to a more far-reaching reduction of the dangers of war. He was, in any case, opposed to unilateral American action. He afterwards put his position in these words:

1. I felt and said emphatically that we should not take military action by air strike or invasion at least until we had used the Organization of American States and the Security Council of the United Nations to bring about the peaceful removal of the threat from nuclear missiles. This is what was done.

2. I favored the quarantine against additional arms shipments to Cuba, but opposed including petrol, oil and lubricants in the first instance. This is what was done.

3. I proposed that in the event that the missiles were rendered inoperable as a result of the OAS-UN proceedings, but had not been withdrawn from the island, that the US should be prepared to negotiate for their withdrawal and for the demilitarization of Cuba by the withdrawal of all Russian forces. And for any such comprehensive result we should be prepared to pay the price in the context of mutual evacuation of bases.*

Stevenson's views on the blockade and use of the UN and the OAS, according to news reports at a later date, were shared by Secretary Rusk, Attorney General Robert Kennedy, and, of course, the President himself. But in the tense atmosphere of the moment, Stevenson's longer range proposals were sidetracked.

At the United Nations Stevenson had another sharp encounter with Russian Delegate Zorin. But this time the roles were reversed. Stevenson was fully and accurately informed,

---

* Letter to the author, March 15, 1963.

while Zorin was in the position of defending unconscionable Soviet action in Cuba by denying that it had taken place. Before a nationwide television audience and with radio coverage throughout the world, Stevenson showed the Security Council photographs of Russian installations which were conclusive evidence that the Soviets had indeed installed missiles capable of carrying nuclear warheads, and directed them toward the United States. Other photographs showed Russian bombers in various stages of uncrating, assembly, or completion. Still other pictures showed additional bases and runways under construction. Zorin, predictably, reminded the Security Council of the last time Stevenson had showed photographs of airplanes, photographs which had turned out to be fraudulent. But this time Stevenson's evidence was so overwhelming and his personal integrity so far beyond question that there was no room for doubt. The American charges against the Soviet Union and Cuba were true. Even as Zorin and the Cuban delegate angrily shouted at Stevenson, Chairman Khrushchev was admitting in letters to President Kennedy that the Soviets had indeed installed nuclear missiles and sent bombers to Cuba—and agreeing, also, to remove them! Khrushchev presently sent Deputy Foreign Minister Kuznetzov to the United Nations to replace Zorin for the Cuba negotiations, thus underscoring the reversal of Russian policy. Among the diplomats at the United Nations it was assumed that Kuznetzov had been chosen because he was known to be on good personal terms with Stevenson.

While Secretary of State Rusk directed American diplomacy in the Organization of American States, Stevenson was in charge of the negotiations at the United Nations. At his request Deputy Secretary of Defense Roswell Gilpatric and John J. McCloy, an eminent Republican and former high government official, were added to his staff to assist in the dealings with the Russians. Gilpatric could speak on technical military matters, while McCloy's presence would show that Stevenson was pressing an American policy supported by both parties. In the negotiations, which were conducted under conditions of great urgency, Stevenson and his advisers succeeded at every point and won the warm acclaim of the delegates from all nations except the Communist bloc. If, in his confrontation with Zorin, Stevenson had shown a spark of indignation, even anger, what was most remarked by the diplomatic corps was the quiet firmness with which he afterwards pressed the American demands for an end to the Russian threat in Cuba. The reaction of the American press was generally enthusiastic about Stevenson's performance. Even representative Republican editors like Alexander Jones of the *Syracuse Herald-Journal*, who had never previously had a kind word for him, now congratulated him. One exception was the *Chicago Tribune*—perhaps for old times' sake!

Not long after the Soviet missiles had been removed, the bases dismantled, and the bombers crated and shipped home, Stevenson was the victim of a political attack reminiscent of the attacks upon him by men like Nixon and McCarthy many years before. In what purported to be revelations of secret meetings in Washington prior to the bockade of Cuba, Stevenson was said to have argued for a line of "appeasement" of the Soviet Union. "Adlai wanted a Munich," an anonymous official was quoted as saying. It was said that he wished to trade American bases in Italy and Turkey for the Russian bases in Cuba. Stevenson immediately denounced the story, which had appeared in the *Saturday Evening Post*, as false in every respect. And he was supported by a remarkable chorus of eminent commentators and national magazines. *Life*, for example, published a feature article defending Stevenson and accusing his accusers of unpardonably irresponsible journalism. The matter was complicated for President Kennedy by the fact that one of the *Post* authors was a close personal friend. Nevertheless the President told his press conference that Stevenson had played a major part in the entire successful enterprise. Later Kennedy released a personal letter to Stevenson warmly thanking him for his efforts and assur-

ing him that he had the fullest confidence of the President.
For his part, Stevenson was satisfied by the President's statements and let the matter rest there. Afterward he suggested
that the whole charge of "appeasement" might have arisen
from a confusion of what he had actually said in the meetings
of the National Security Council:

> I think the confusion arose because somebody interpreted
> my position as offering to trade a base in exchange
> for rendering the missiles inoperable, i.e. removing the
> gun from our head, rather than the larger package of re-
> moving the Russians from Cuba. But obviously the US
> has long pursued a policy of refusing to negotiate under
> threat and I had no such idea at the time.*

For Stevenson, as for the nation, there was deep irony in
the whole unpleasant episode. Less than three months later
the Department of Defense announced that it was disman-
tling the American bases in Turkey—with no *quid pro quo*
from the Russians such as Stevenson had proposed. And the
Russians remained firmly entrenched in Cuba, perhaps because
the Administration had been willing to go only a part of the
way Stevenson had urged.

V

THE MOST POIGNANT MOMENT of Stevenson's career in the
United Nations came when he spoke for his country at the
special session of the General Assembly honoring the memory of John Fitzgerald Kennedy. In the years of his service
under President Kennedy, Stevenson had grown closer, not
more distant, to the young President, and had come to respect
his leadership deeply. Stevenson believed that Kennedy had
been on the way to genuine greatness as an American and
world figure. The President's death in Dallas, coming only a
few days after he had himself been attacked by a group of

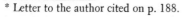
* Letter to the author cited on p. 188.

hecklers in the same city, shocked Stevenson more, perhaps, than any event of his lifetime.

On November 26, 1963, at the United Nations, Stevenson spoke of Kennedy in words more charged with feeling than any ceremonial eulogy. "President Kennedy was so contemporary a man," he said, "so involved in our world—so immersed in our times—so responsive to its challenges—so intense a participant in the great events and great decisions of our day, that he seemed the very symbol of the vitality and the exuberance that is the essence of life itself." Stevenson went on to underline the things about Kennedy he believed to be most memorable:

> We shall not soon forget the late President's driving ambition for his own country—his concept of a permanently dynamic society spreading abundance to the last corner of this land, and extending justice, tolerance and dignity to all of its citizens alike.

> We shall not soon forget that he held fast to the vision of a world in which the peace is secure; in which inevitable conflicts are reconciled by pacific means; in which nations devote their energies to the welfare of all their citizens; and in which the vast and colorful diversity of human society can flourish in a restless, competitive search for a better society.

> We shall not soon forget that by word and by deed he gave proof of profound confidence in the present value and the future promise of this great organization, the United Nations.

Finally, he spoke of the unknowable difference Kennedy's death would make:

> Now he is gone. Today we mourn him. Tomorrow and tomorrow we shall miss him. And so we shall never know how different the world might have been had fate

permitted this blazing talent to live and labor longer at man's unfinished agenda for peace and progress for all.

As for the future, Stevenson presently informed the United Nations that he had been "directed to affirm" that there would be "no Johnson policy toward the United Nations—any more than there was a Kennedy policy. There was —and is—only a United States policy. And that outlasts violence and outlives men."

President Lyndon B. Johnson immediately asked Stevenson to remain at his post. Stevenson agreed without hesitation, both because he shared the new President's desire to maintain American stability and continuity of policy during the critical months of readjustment, and because he wished to be of use to an old friend whose ability he respected and whose difficult position he fully appreciated. President Johnson, for his part, reciprocated by giving Stevenson his full confidence and making him, as Kennedy had done, one of his small group of close advisers.*

As a member of the Johnson Administration, Stevenson's main assignment was to defend United States policy in Vietnam and in Santo Domingo. Neither was an easy task for a man of peace. But he could console himself that it was at least as difficult for the President. In Vietnam, Stevenson repeatedly told the UN, the United States was fighting to help a small nation maintain its political integrity against Communist aggression. To leave that small nation to its fate would be to invite similar aggression elsewhere in Southeast Asia and, perhaps, in other parts of the world. If there was no likely military solution to the issue drawn in Vietnam, it was nevertheless necessary to answer every military advance or thrust by military means until the Communists could be persuaded to go to the conference table.

As a well-loved friend of Latin America and a long-time

---

* Stevenson to the author, August 14, 1964.

opponent of the old "big stick" policies of Theodore Roosevelt, Stevenson regretted the necessity for United States intervention in the Dominican Republic in April, 1965. But he was entirely persuaded that vigorous action was necessary to restore order and to forestall the emergence of a second Castro-type government in Central America. In the United Nations he explained the American action in terms of the principles of freedom and self-determination, worked tirelessly to hold together the Latin American delegations in a common front to defend the OAS against Soviet denunciation, and succeeded in allaying in some measure the fears of the neutral bloc nations that the United States might be returning to a long discarded policy of trying to play strong man in Inter-American affairs.

If there was any important failure in Stevenson's five year record as American Representative at the United Nations, it was in his persistent but unrewarding effort during the General Assembly of 1965 to persuade the Soviet Union, France, Belgium, and some other nations, to pay, at least in part, their financial dues to the UN. The issue was whether, under the Charter, nations which were opposed to certain peacekeeping operations of the UN could withhold their financial support. The Soviet Union, for example, was opposed to the UN operation in the Congo, as was Belgium. Article 19 provided that after two years of financial arrears a country would automatically lose its vote in the Assembly. It was American policy to hold to this provision on the ground that if it were not enforced the UN executive effort, at least, would be frustrated. This, of course, was precisely the intention of the Soviet Union, as it had been in the matter of the election of the Secretary General three years before. Stevenson was never entirely certain how a vote would come out if the issue were squarely faced by the Assembly. And he was fully conscious, as was President Johnson, of the fact that the UN could not effectively function without the Soviet Union. Under these circumstances, Stevenson sought to find an acceptable compromise formula. One suggestion was that the

Soviet Union and other delinqent nations might make "voluntary contributions" to UN agencies of which they approved —like UNICEF—and have them credited to their delinquent peacekeeping accounts. Negotiations on this possibility extended throughout the session, but were eventually suspended without a decision.

Meanwhile, Stevenson cooperated, on behalf of the United States, in the transparent but necessary device of conducting all the Assembly's business without a formal vote. It was an exhausting session, and Stevenson was glad, when it was over, to go in June to Geneva for the less tense meetings of the Economic and Social Council. He was returning home by way of London on July 14 when, without prior hint of illness, he collapsed and died while taking an afternoon walk near the United States Embassy. Only a few moments before he had completed taping a radio program for the BBC defending American policy in Vietnam. After listening to the tape, both Embassy and BBC officials decided to go ahead with the broadcast. Thus, in a peculiarly appropriate way, Governor Stevenson continued to speak for his country and for human freedom even after his death.

VI

WHILE IT IS MUCH TOO EARLY to judge the historic impact of Adlai Stevenson's role in the United Nations, it is already clear that his record of achievement during the Kennedy and Johnson Administrations, from 1961 to mid-1965, was unparalleled.

By skillfully blending his advantage as spokesman for the most powerful of the free nations with his personal talents as a patient negotiator relying upon reason, he went far toward restoring the image of the United States as the "friend and aider" of those who would live in freedom. He was not content merely to "stand up to the Russians," but insisted that

the United States must always present itself as the voice of
a genuine democratic alternative to Communism. This meant
that in the General Assembly Stevenson would side, on certain sharply drawn issues, with the ex-colonial states, even
against some of America's western allies. When he did so, as
in criticizing the role of the Portuguese in Angola, it was, of
course, with the full support of the President. But to the
Afro-Asian representatives, Stevenson's words carried more
than the formal assurances of his nation. They knew that
Adlai Stevenson would not be sitting in the American delegate's chair unless he himself were satisfied of American sincerity.

To Stevenson more than to any other individual the
United Nations owes the continuing strength of its executive
branch. His resourceful leadership in preserving the Secretary
General's office from ruin by the Russian troika plan has been
acknowledged all over the world. His firm support of the Secretary General, first Hammarskjöld and afterwards U Thant,
in the Congo crisis played an important part in the ultimate
restoration of order in that troubled area. And Stevenson's
patient firmness in dealing with the Russians during the Cuba
crisis of 1962 had, for a time at least, the effect of altering the
cold war line of the Soviet Union at the United Nations. The
replacement of Zorin brought an end to the use of the Security Council and the General Assembly as sounding boards
for Russian abuse and vilification of the West. If little progress was made toward resolution of the great issues that divided East and West, at least the manners of the representatives were once again civilized.

But no one understood better than Adlai Stevenson himself that a diplomat is no more effective, in the final analysis,
than the power and wisdom of his government and country.
This was why he insisted, as a condition for accepting his
post at the United Nations, that he share in the process of
formulating American foreign policy. He could not be content to act simply as a formal spokesman for policies made by

others. Popular expectation was too high for that. Circumstances, and his own abilities and character, had made him a statesman. As a statesman he will be judged. His personal achievement was distinguished by any standard. But his place in history, as he played his part on the world stage at the United Nations, was irrevocably tied to the destiny of the country he loved to serve.

VII

DURING HIS YEARS at the United Nations Adlai Stevenson had many honors thrust upon him, not as an official but for his own sake. He continued to receive many more invitations to speak at university commencements than he could possibly accept. His list of honorary degrees rivaled that of the late Robert Frost, who is said to have established an all time record.

One honor brought him a special satisfaction. Friends at the Jewish Theological Seminary established the Adlai E. Stevenson Foundation to advance ethical understanding among nations through a program of scholarships to graduate students of divinity and philosophy. At the founding dinner Stevenson spoke eloquently on this subject, close to his heart for years and now a central part of his work as a world statesman:

> . . . I see a great opportunity here to further the search for those enduring values which transcend the divisive frictions between nations. While each country supports its national interests through an ethical rationalization, human progress can only be achieved if a way is found to identify the ethical ideas which are the basis for long range goals helpful to all men.

"I am proud and grateful," he said, "to be identified with such healing scholarship."

In November, 1962 Mrs. Eleanor Roosevelt on her deathbed asked to see Adlai Stevenson for one brief, final visit. This revered "First Lady of the World" had sponsored his public career from the time of their serving together in the United Nations just after World War II. She had often said that Stevenson spoke the American conscience and the American aspiration better than any other man of the time. When she died, Stevenson's word of tribute was among the briefest yet most moving of all the messages that came from the leading statesmen of the world: "She would rather light candles," he said, "than curse the darkness; and her glow has warmed the world." Soon afterwards he assumed responsibility for charting the course of the new Eleanor Roosevelt Foundation.

Among his other civic activities, aside from his duties at the UN, Stevenson served as President of the Field Foundation; trustee of the Woodrow Wilson Foundation; trustee of several universities. He was also a member of numerous national boards and conference committees devoted to advancing international understanding and the cause of peace. Every other Sunday in 1961 and 1962 he conducted a nationwide television program, "Adlai Stevenson Reports," in which he interviewed visiting statesmen and held conversations with guests on world problems. Though he joked occasionally about his advancing years his staff could testify that Stevenson in his sixties was hardly less energetic and demanding of himself than he had been in his forties when he first took a prominent place in public life.

Stevenson was, in fact, so vigorous and still so much in the public mind that his name was immediately introduced into political speculation after the death of President Kennedy. A grassroots attempt was made to "draft Stevenson for Vice President," and the opinion polls showed that he would be the choice of a great many Democrats. Stevenson's reaction to this new flurry of activity was simply that he would not under any circumstances seek the nomination, that he assumed President Johnson would wish to choose a younger man, but that he would serve if called upon. He refused thereafter even to discuss the matter. His name, however, continued to figure in newspaper speculation and political gossip, until the President, in June 1964, announced that he would not select any member of his cabinet to be his running mate.

Meanwhile the Democrats of New York approached Stevenson with the proposal that he run for the Senate from that state. He was flattered. Most of his life was then being lived in New York City, and he had always had a strong following there both among the Democrats and in the Liberal Party. Further, he had always had an interest in the Senate as a place to make his ideas known and influential. But he had no longer any enthusiasm for campaigning and no ambition to return to the political wars. He declined with warm thanks. The statesman would stay at his post as statesman.

And it was as elder statesman that he appeared at the 1964 Democratic Convention in Atlantic City. His role was not a part of the political proceedings, but to pay tribute to Mrs. Roosevelt on behalf of the national Democratic Party. As he stood on the rostrum, the audience gave him a standing ovation. He waved and smiled, somewhat uncomfortably, then quickly signalled for silence. Mrs. Roosevelt, he told the Convention, had been the "conscience of the Democratic Party." Now that she had gone, the party would do well to remember her admonitions to consult always the right course, not the expedient. From her example, Stevenson said, not only Democrats but all Americans and all people everywhere could learn the lessons of humility, charity, and magnanimity. "She thought of herself as an ugly duckling," he said, "but she walked in beauty in the ghettoes of the world." The beauty and the propriety of the tribute underscored Stevenson's own spiritual and political kinship to Mrs. Roosevelt. To his hearers it was clear, without need to state it, that Stevenson was himself the voice of conscience replacing the voice that had been stilled.

"Governor" Stevenson (even as Ambassador he preferred the old courtesy title) had as full and useful a life as any statesman of his time. In his own country few men in the twentieth century have so remarkable a record of achievement. If he could not be President, it is already clear that his contribution to the well-being of his country, to the advancement of its ideals and principles, and his influence toward peace in the world cannot be matched by any other defeated candidate for the American Presidency. Perhaps history will decide that, in an important sense, Adlai E. Stevenson was never defeated at all.

"The world of freedom and human dignity," said President Johnson, "has lost its most articulate champion; America has lost its most eloquent voice."

After a national memorial service in Washington, Stevenson was taken to Springfield, Illinois to lie in state at the Capitol, while tens of thousands of people paid final respects to one of the greatest sons of Illinois. The catafalque had, appropriately, been Lincoln's; it had not been used since April, 1865. At the graveside in the cemetery at Bloomington, the Unitarian minister spoke a few simple words. "Governor Stevenson," he said, "has ended his long and patient quest for the peace of the world. He has come home to Illinois."

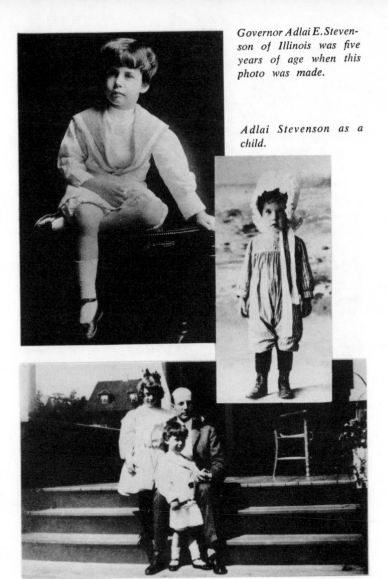

Governor Adlai E. Stevenson of Illinois was five years of age when this photo was made.

Adlai Stevenson as a child.

Governor Adlai E. Stevenson with his father, Lewis G. Stevenson, and his sister Elizabeth (now Mrs. Ernest Ives of Bloomington, Illinois). The photograph was taken at Charlevoix, Michigan, during a summer vacation.

Birthplace of Governor Stevenson
Adlai Stevenson was born in this house on the Southwest side of Los Angeles, Calif., in 1900. The neighborhood was then one of the city's very best. The house has since been sold several times and is now a rooming house. Governor Stevenson was born in the master bedroom at upper right and lived here until he was nearly six.

Adlai Stevenson is shown in three phases of his career as a student. At left is young Adlai at the age of ten when he attended the Washington Street School in Bloomington, Illinois. In center he is shown at the age of 15 as a pupil of University High School, Normal, Illinois. At right he's shown as a graduate of North Western University Law School in 1926.

The Governor Tries His Hand
Doffing their coats on a tour of the Chicago Railroad Fair on Illinois Day Aug. 8, 1949 Governor Adlai Stevenson and Major Lenox R. Lohr, President of The Fair, try out a section gang handcar from the "Wheels a Rolling" Pageant.

A Wave from the Governor
Wearing an American Legion cap, Gov. Adlai Stevenson waves to his audience before addressing the 1952 Legion Convention in Madison Square Garden, New York.

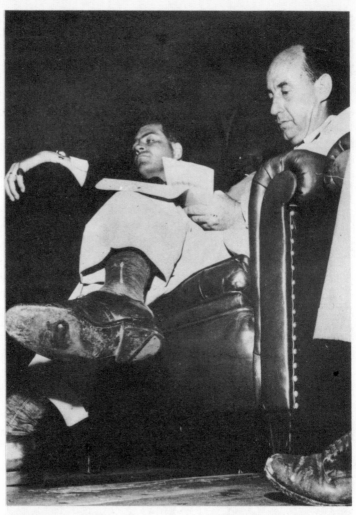

1952 Campaign Shoe
Governor Adlai Stevenson, Democrat nominee for President bares
a worn sole to his Labor Day rally audience in Flint, Michigan.
Michigan's Governor, G. Mennen Williams, looks worn from the
whirlwind politics-and-labor tour that took in five Michigan cities
in 12 hours.

Governor Adlai E. Stevenson receives a box of grapes during 1952 campaign in California.

Adlai Cleans Up
The Democratic Presidential Nominee brushes off plaque on back of his campaign train at Springfield, Illinois, before leaving on final stumping trip before the election. Watching are his Aunt, Letitia Stevenson (left) and his sister, Mrs. Ernest Ives.

Adlai Stevenson, made a short visit to Indo-China in March 1953. At the residence of the Bishop of Phat Diem, facing camera, l. to r.: Mr. Stevenson, the Bishop of Phat Diem, Monsignor Le Huu Tu, and Gen. Gonzales De Linares, Commander in Chief in North Vietnam.

Adlai Stevenson called on Prime Minister Shigeru Yoshide at his official residence. As the photographer suggested that the diminutive Yoshida stand in the middle of the trio, Stevenson quipped: "that's right, always put a politician in the middle." (left to right: U. S. Ambassador Robert Murphy; Yoshida; Stevenson.)

Stevenson Decked Out to Hit the Deck
Stevenson and Lt. Gen. Maxwell D. Taylor, Commander of the 8th Army, smile encouragement at one another as they prepare to board navy dive bomber for flight from Korea to flight deck of the aircraft carrier USS Oriskany.

Receive Honorary Degrees
Adlai E. Stevenson and Harvard President Nathan M. Pusey walk
in academic procession enroute to the 207th annual commencement
exercises of Princeton University, June 15, 1954. Both received Honor-
ary Doctor of Laws Degrees. The former Governor of Illinois, was
a graduate of the Princeton Class of 1922.

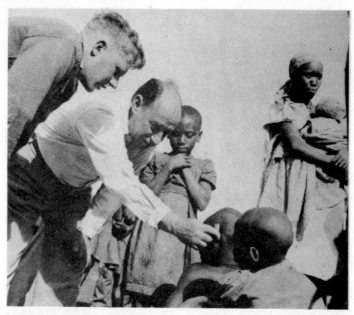

Adlai Stevenson in Kenya
*Adlai Stevenson, arrived in Nairobi April 22, 1955 for a short visit
to Kenya. Here he admires the earrings of Kikuyu women at the
Kikuyu reserve in the Kiambu district.*

*Stevenson meets Chief
Kabunyi Muragami, head
of the local African tri-
bunal.*

L. to R. Adlai Stevenson Jr., Adlai Stevenson, John Fell Stevenson 2nd, and Mrs. Adlai Stevenson, Jr. during the 1956 presidential campaign.

In Chicago, Adlai Stevenson, waves both arms in greeting to his cheering audience at the ampitheatre where he was nominated by the 1956 Democratic National Convention.

Sen. Estes Kefauver, Democratic vice presidential nominee, points to a map as he and Adlai Stevenson, the party's candidate for president, go over 1956 campaign routes.

Good for More than Bottles
An empty bottle case is used for the platform "elevator" at the
New York State Liberal Party Convention at the Manhattan Center,
New York. Stevenson, stepping to the podium, is about to accept
the party's nomination for President.

Governor Stevenson and Senator Hubert Humphrey from Minnesota.

A Pretty Greeting for Stevenson
The Democratic presidential nominee finds himself surrounded by a group of pretty supporters on hand to greet him when he arrived at LaGuardia airport, New York City.

Newcomer on Reviewing Stand
Dana De Friedberg, four, of Asbury Park, New Jersey, dressed in a Polish costume, sits on rail of reviewing stand for the annual Pulaski Day Parade in New York. On the occasion she met Adlai Stevenson, and New York's Mayor Robert Wagner.

In The Spotlight
Stevenson, under the glare of lights, speaks before a Democratic party rally in New York's Madison Square Garden.

Small Talk — Big Crowd
Mrs. Eleanor Roosevelt and Adlai Stevenson make small talk on
the rostrum before the crowd of the Democratic Party Rally in
New York's Madison Square Garden.

Confetti Storm
Using his hand to protect his eyes, the 1956 Democratic presidential candidate is greeted by a confetti-throwing crowd while entering Mechanics Building in Boston where he made a nationally televised speech. Stevenson's son, Adlai, Jr., is in background.

Stevenson Visits Dr. Schweitzer
Adlai Stevenson poses alongside Dr. Albert Schweitzer during a three-day visit with the world-famous philosopher at his hospital in Lamberene, French Equatorial Africa.

Adlai Stevenson Presents his Credentials
New permanent representative of the United States to the United Nations presents his credentials to Secretary-General Dag Hammarskjold.

Adlai Relaxes with Relatives
During his visit to old home town, Bloomington, Illinois, United
Nations Ambassador Adlai Stevenson romped with youngsters of
his nephew Timmothy Ives. With "Uncle Ad" are Sandra (left),
Tim (right), and Alison.

Here for Report on Congo
Adlai Stevenson, U. S. Ambassador to the United Nations, reaches arm towards President John F. Kennedy as they arrive at New York's Hotel Carlyle. The President flew in from Buffalo, N. Y., to hear Stevenson's report on the Congo situation.

Thinking Ahead

Wasting no time, Adlai Stevenson works on a speech for the next day as a meeting of the United Nations Security Council breaks up. Seated at the head of the council table, Stevenson faces two signs—United States to mark the U. S. delegate, and President to identify him as the holder of the rotating position.

Listens to Both Sides
The U. S. Ambassador to the United Nations expresses views at
the United Nations Security Council Meeting as Patrick Dean, left,
listens. In center photo Stevenson listens to Orhan Eralp of Turkey.
Later, in bottom photo, Stevenson confers with Dimitri Bitsios, of
Greece, as Charles Yost listens between them.

Stevenson Hears Soviet Attack U.S. at U.N.
The Chief U.S. Delegate to the United Nations presented this pensive
study at the Security Council session in New York. He's shown as he
heard Soviet Delegate Nikolai Federenko attack the U.S.-Belgium
Rescue Mission to the Congo.

When Ike Hosted Adlai at the White House
Adlai E. Stevenson and President Eisenhower shook hands at the
White House in February of 1953 when Stevenson lunched with
Eisenhower and a group of congressmen.

Stevenson Just Before He Died
This is the last known photo taken of the late Ambassador Adlai Stevenson. The picture was taken on July 14, 1965 as he was leaving the American Embassy Building in London. Stevenson fell to the pavement moments after picture was taken. He was certified dead on arrival at St. George's Hospital in the British Capital.

Pay Homage to Stevenson
President and Mrs. Johnson, escorted by churchmen, walk near "The Great Crossing" of Washington Cathedral, where the flag-covered coffin of Adlai Stevenson rests for memorial service. The Johnsons headed 2,000 mourners who attended the final Washington rites for the U. N. ambassador.

Our Broken Mainspring

(*Lecture in memory of* A. *Powell Davies, Constitution Hall, January, 1959.*)

It is hard indeed to pay adequate homage in words to a man whose own words were so fresh, so apt and fitting to the important issues of the day.

But I am encouraged by one fact. Dr. A. Powell Davies did not feel that his office as a minister of religion debarred him from comment upon contemporary problems. On the contrary, he saw that he could make his message relevant to his people only by showing it at work in the concrete issues of their daily lives.

I think of a story my grandfather Stevenson, a devout Scotch-Presbyterian, told about the preacher who was driving along a back road in the South when he espied a parishioner wearily clearing up a poor, stony field. "That's a fine job you and the Lord have done clearing up that rocky field," he shouted. "Thank you, parson," the man replied. "But I wish you could have seen it when the Lord had it all to himself."

Dr. Davies believed that God is dependent on man, as man is on God. He believed that the clergy above all were responsible for making a reality of the bond between God and man, and he was fearless in letting his congregation and the world know the truth as he saw it. He had a sensitive awareness of peril to the individual in our day of bigness, of statism and conformity. Therefore he was impelled to fight for the oppressed and the persecuted; to fight for equal justice for all and the rights inherent in our citizenship. Ardently he defended freedom of the mind, free speech, the right of the dissenter to speak, the duty of the conformist to listen. And his compassion was boundless.

It was the tardiness of the American social conscience in understanding the severity of its ordeal, its contest with authoritarianism that made Dr. Davies impatient, that made him work so hard to awaken us to the perils. He literally wore himself out trying to mobilize public opinion, trying to induce every American to hold himself personally responsible for the preservation of freedom.

From the mountain of his vision, Dr. Davies constantly proclaimed the political relevance of moral principle and of religion as a "judgment of righteousness." From the dusty plain of politics I would like in my turn to reaffirm this relevance. I like to believe that there may be some value in echoing testimony from a layman who has spent his middle life in the press and confusion of great events—in government service, in diplomacy and in politics.

There is a phrase of Dr. Davies that stays in my mind. I do not know when I have heard a more terse and pregnant summing up of our predicament. "The world," he said, "is now too dangerous for anything but the truth, too small for anything but brotherhood." This I believe to be in broad measure a correct estimate of the condition of human society, which is now capable, with a few hydrogen bombs, of extinguishing itself. Today we can all be killed by the same bombs or atomic fallout. In that sense we have attained a desperate physical solidarity. But moral and social solidarity in the family of man is still to be found.

Not so long ago I visited Dr. Albert Schweitzer in his primitive jungle hospital in French Equatorial Africa, and he told me that he considered this the most dangerous period in history. I said, "In contemporary history?" "No," he said, "in all human history." "Why?" "Because," he said, "heretofore nature has controlled man in the last analysis, but now man has learned to control elemental forces of nature—before he has learned to control himself."

Many of us seem, here in our country, to rely on some mythical God-given superiority of the white Western world to save us. And my concern is that there is more evidence that the Communists accept the reality of the human condition than we do.

It is impossible to spend weeks traveling around the Soviet Union, as I did this summer, without taking away an overwhelming impression of thrust and purpose in most aspects of Soviet life. The revolutionary ardor of the early days to be sure has cooled with time but even the very pragmatic political leaders seem to believe profoundly in the truth of their way of life and are quietly confident that it will sweep the whole world in time. I think they sincerely believe that their methods, their aspirations, their dreams, make up the final truth about the nature of man and society; that collective man in the collective state is the ultimate unfolding of human destiny, the end of history, the "far-off divine event" for which mankind has been in long travail, the vision of "all things made new" that has haunted men's minds ever since Christianity thrust into human thought the intoxicating ideal of a perfected humanity.

From this conviction, if I have not overstated it, flow two consequences. The first is that no effort, no dedication, no sacrifice is too great that may help to realize the Communist party's goals in Soviet society. The second is that no corner of humanity can be a matter of indifference to the Communists, because the whole human race is destined to become in time one communist brotherhood.

The energy, the drive, the dedication in the U.S.S.R. spill over into international affairs in ways that we are only now beginning to realize. In part, of course, this is the restless concern which all imperial powers must exercise, especially when the peoples they control are as restive and unreliable as the captive peoples in Russia's European empire. But Communist activity, planning and efforts in trade and aid are not confined to areas of Communist control. They are world-wide, and there is no corner of the earth's surface which the Russians think too insignificant for their attention, none.

All this we know—or begin to know. But I wonder how often we try to grasp the scale of dedication that lies behind it. Why should they be so busy? Why so much work and thought? Why such diversion of precious resources? Why such patience through every setback, such forward thrusts through every point of Western weakness? Heaven knows, we only want to stay home. Why don't they? Why do we never meet an isolationist Communist? These are some of the questions that haunted me when I confronted at first hand this iron, forceful, formidable way of life.

And I do not think that there is any doubt about the answer. Part of it is simply needed foreign trade. Part is fear, the search for security through friends. And part is the historical centrifugal forces in Russia which have been pressing outward for two hundred years—to the Pacific, the Balkans, the Middle East, the Straits, and so on. But the important thing is that the Soviet Russians believe in their truth, as the men of the Western world once believed in theirs. They, not we, are firing the shots that are heard round the world—and also the satellites that orbit above it. The fact that their faith is in many ways an evil perversion of the great propositions that once made the blood course in Western veins does not alter the fact that their tempo is dynamic and rapid, ours sluggish—even, I think, to ourselves.

Surely, the reason cannot be that we Americans have lost our vision of truth and brotherhood. No country on earth owes the sense of community more explicitly to the fact that it is united not by race or nationality but by fidelity to an idea. We were born "dedicated to a proposition" and our greatest leaders—the Jeffersons, the Lincolns, the Wilsons—were not great because they achieved purely American purposes, but because they were able to speak for humanity at large and extend their vision to the whole family of man.

Nor, I believe, can we find fault with the substance of

what we have endearingly called the American dream. Its truths are still "self-evident." The possession of liberty and the pursuit of happiness—rightly understood—these have not been overthrown as the highest goods of human society. Indeed, the ferment of our freedom works inexorably and dangerously in the Communist world. No one can have visited Poland without seeing how little the Polish people really accept their servitude and how they look beyond their neighbors to the free world as the reservoir of power and of hope.

But, alas, on the basis of the record, one would hardly suspect that the Western world possessed so powerful a weapon. Our talk—in diplomacy, in strategy, in aid and trade, in all of the intricacies of our world-wide relations—has been to a depressing degree purely defensive. We have offered aid not to help others but to shield ourselves. We have reacted to countless Soviet initiatives; acted on our own initiative barely at all. We watch the skies for other people's Sputniks and listen to the telegraph wires for other people's moves. Yet we are the free men of this universe; we are the children of liberty, the beneficiaries of unequaled abundance, and heirs of the highest, proudest political tradition ever known to man!

Why this lack of initiative? Why this paralysis of will? What have we done to our truth, our brotherhood—the supreme truth of freedom, the Christian truth of brotherly love? Have they failed? Or have we?

There is no more urgent duty than to discover why we have failed, if we have, and I think we have, and to get back into the arena, aspiring, striving, fighting, if you please, once more for what we believe. An examination of what you might call our collective conscience is to my mind far more important than particular projects or programs. You can have a perfect assembly of pieces in your watch, but they are worthless if the mainspring is broken. I am not worried about our various pieces—our technology, our science, our machines, our resources. But I am concerned, desperately concerned, about our mainspring. That it has run down, we know. But is it broken; is it broken beyond repair? In the last analysis, no question is worth more consideration in America today.

And I would like to suggest some of the ways in which it seems to me we have enfeebled the great central pulse of our freedom, the great truth of liberty, which, more than any other nation, we first set working in the modern world.

Goethe, who also lived through a crisis of freedom, said to his generation: "What you have inherited from your fathers, earn over again for yourselves or it will not be yours." We inherited this freedom we talk about so glibly. We seem unaware that it has to be remade and re-earned in each generation of man. One reason for this failure is, I believe, passing at last. In recent years we were stifled with complacent self-confidence. We believed ourselves dominant in every field. We talked of "the American Century." We forgot the ardors and the efforts that had given us a measure of pre-eminence. Complacency made us impervious to ideas, even the obvious idea that we are in danger. So we assumed that all we needed was to sit still and enjoy the "peace and prosperity" that was our right.

I believe that phase is now passing. Our foolish languor has been shaken, if not shattered. We are more ready to examine ourselves and our record. And it is a privilege of our society that every citizen should make his own inquiry. If I stress one or the other aspect of the problem, this is simply my angle of vision. You will have yours. The urgent thing is to feel the need for re-thinking and to set to work the ultimate energies of a free society—which cannot be done by the fiat of government but only by the troubled conscience of responsible men and women.

I believe—as I have said before—that we have confused the free with the free and easy. If freedom had been the happy, simple, relaxed state of ordinary humanity, man would have everywhere been free—whereas through most of time and space he has been in chains. Do not let us make any mistake about this. The natural government of man is servitude.

Tyranny is the normal pattern of government. It is only by intense thought, by great effort, by burning idealism and unlimited sacrifice that freedom has prevailed as a system of government. And the efforts which were first necessary to create it are fully as necessary to sustain it in our own day.

He who offers this thing that we call freedom as the soft option is a deceiver or himself deceived. He who sells it cheap or offers it as the by-product of this or that economic system is knave or fool. For freedom demands infinitely more care and devotion than any other political system. It puts consent and personal initiative in the place of command and obedience. By relying upon the devotion and initiative of ordinary citizens, it gives up the harsh but effective disciplines that underpin all the tyrannies which over the millennia have stunted the full stature of man.

But of what use is escape from external restraint if given the opportunity man simply stunts himself? If freedom means ease alone, if it means shirking the hard disciplines of learning, if it means evading the rigors and rewards of creative activity, if it means more expenditure on advertising than on education, if it means "bachelor cooking" and "life adjustment" courses in the schools, and the steady cult of the trivial and the mediocre, if it means—worst of all—indifference, even contempt for all but athletic excellence in our educational system, we may keep for a time the forms of free society, but its spirit will be dead.

I believe we have had enough of adjustment, of conformity, of easy options and the least common denominator in our system. We need instead to see the "pursuit of happiness" in terms which are historically proven and psychologically correct. The dreary failure in history of all classes committed to pleasure and profit alone, the vacuity and misery accompanying the sole pursuit of ease—the collapse of the French aristocracy, the corruption of imperial Rome, the decline and fall of the resplendent Manchus—all these facts of history do not lose their point because the pleasures of today are mass pleasures and no longer the enjoyments of an elite. If we become a nation of Bourbons, numbers will not save us. We shall go their way, too. Vacuity and indifference are not redeemed by the fact that everyone can share in them. They merely restrict the circle from which regeneration can come.

I say this—I hope you will believe me—in no Puritan or pleasure-hating spirit. On the contrary, there is no boredom, no misery to equal the pursuit of distraction alone. We do not slip into happiness. It is strenuously sought and earned. A nation glued to recreation, to the television screen, is not simply at a loss before the iron pioneers of the new collective society. It is not even having a good time. No society has ever spent as much as we do on drink and tranquilizers. Can one argue that this is evidence of universal fun? I ran across a quotation from La Bruyère on the court of Louis XIV which struck me as relevant: "Les joies sont visibles, mais fausses, et les chagrins cachés, mais réels"—its joys are visible, but artificial, and its sorrows hidden, but real.

But perhaps this misunderstanding of the true nature of happiness and of the conditions of its pursuit is simply an aspect of something else—our misunderstanding of the real nature of freedom. I recall the words of the wise Judge Learned Hand, who warned us that freedom would not survive in our Constitution if it had already died in the hearts of the people. We shall not have a free society unless we have free men.

And how often do we reflect upon what this inner freedom entails? "Give me the man," cries Hamlet, "who is not passion's slave." But this is what we are in danger of becoming, slaves to a tyranny more intimate and inescapable than any that Stalin or Mao Tse-tung could impose. We can be made slaves simply by the clutter and complexity of modern living—which notoriously leaves no time for serious thought and offers every means of distraction so that we can avoid such thought. Between aircraft that take us everywhere more rapidly, newspapers that grow in weight and coverage, news that flashes round the globe, ceaseless and competitive entertainment, fashions—God help us!—that change from sack to trapeze and back again, we can fill up every "unforgiving minute" with enough trash and preoccupation to still forever the deeper voices of the soul. Like Matthew Arnold, we can

". . . see all sights from pole to pole,
  And glance and nod and hustle by,
And never once possess our soul
      Before we die."

How are we to defend freedom if, for the tyranny of external control we substitute the clattering, cluttering tyranny of internal aimlessness and fuss? This freedom of our souls, freedom at the profoundest level of our being, is not a gift to us by our contemporary way of life. On the contrary, much of this life is a direct conspiracy against it. And if we cannot —by certain discipline, by readiness for reflection and quiet, by determination to do the difficult and aim at a lasting good—rediscover the real purpose and direction of our existence, we shall not be free. Our society will not be free. And between a chaotic, selfish, indifferent, commercial society and the iron discipline of the Communist world, I would not like to predict the outcome. Outer tyranny with purpose may well triumph over the inner, purposeless tyranny of a confused and aimless way of life.

I doubt if any society in history has faced so great a moral challenge as ours, or needed more desperately to draw on the deepest sources of courage and responsibility. Ours is the first human community in which resources are so abundant that almost no policies lie beyond our capacity for purely physical reasons. What we decide to do, we can do. The inhibitions of poverty—lack of resources, lack of capital, lack of power—do not hold us back. We can accomplish what we aim at. Thus perhaps for the first time in the world, choice, not means, ends, not instruments, are decisive.

Then again we have proved—drably and dangerously—over the last decade that defensiveness is not a sufficient reason for action. All the policies we have pursued in self-defense have left us still on the defensive. But if we do not act from fear, we must find some other motivation. In free society there is no other alternative but to tap the vigor, the faith, the imagination of the people themselves. We must find out once more who we are, as the psychologists say.

But perhaps the most urgent reason why the quality of our moral response has become the decisive issue in politics is quite simply that most of the major problems of our day present themselves in moral terms, and are probably insoluble without some stirring of generosity, some measure of vision. Let me give you three instances. In the wealthiest nation in the world, at least five million families still live in squalid but remediable poverty. They are a minority. They do not have the votes to force the issue of their misfortune into the front rank of public issues. They depend, for remedies, upon the alert conscience of the majority. But how do we keep the conscience sensitive and alert? By concentrating on our own concerns? By adding the dishwasher to the television set to the air conditioner? By griping over taxes and attacking that great bogey we call "the welfare state"? By closing our minds every time our shiny car takes us through a slum? No—we shall have the dedication, the drive to wipe poverty out of this rich land only if the well-to-do majority of today do not repeat the selfish indifference which, in many communities, has been the epitaph of the well-to-do of yesterday.

Or take the issue of the rights and status of our colored citizens. This is our small share of a world-wide problem. The four hundred years of dominance of men of white skin is ending. The vast colored majority of mankind are seeking the opportunity and the respect which white people have been lucky enough to enjoy for so long—sometimes at the colored people's expense. But, within this world-wide crisis, we in America, with our colored minority, have a major role to play—for good or evil. "The unfinished work" which Lincoln left us, of creating a society in which all men can hold up their heads as equals and self-respecting citizens, can never be accomplished unless there are enough white men and women who resist to the core of their being the moral evil of treating any of God's children as essentially inferior.

Nor is this simply a question of our own, national community. I come back to the painful fact that the Communists show a world-wide concern which is largely lacking among the men of the West. The whole human race is their horizon. Their "brotherhood" is materialist, collectivist, atheist, and we dislike it, but it embraces everybody, and it is the framework of policies which take the missionaries of their new order to the ends of the earth. I say with all the emphasis that I can command that we have no corresponding commitment to our fellow man. For hundreds of years, we have preached the Christian promise of brotherhood, but today, when vanishing space and scientific revolution have turned our planet into a single neighborhood, the ideal means little in terms of concern or conviction, in terms of policy or of action.

Here we are in the Atlantic world, 16 percent of the world's peoples consuming 70 percent of the world's wealth. We cannot be indifferent to the moral implications of this gigantic gap. I do not know how we can gain a new perspective about the narrow world of plenty and of poverty in which we live unless moral insights of justice and compassion stir us to understand the privileged position in which we live.

We are not going to be stirred to action by our own needs. We are the cushioned, the protected, the fortunate minority. It is not the measure of our morals or the lesson of our history to be spurred on only by fear of Russian encroachment. What we have done has largely been from this motivation, and it has left us on the defensive. Our hope is to accept the implications of our own faith, to make concrete the image of brotherhood which we profess, to set to work to express our dedication in whatever effort or sacrifice the world's needs may dictate. And, if we must always think in terms of contest with the Soviets, let us bear in mind that the ability to create the good life for the greatest numbers will be decisive.

This age has been defined in many ways—as a time of conflict in ideology, as a time of ferment in technology, as a period of revolution in science, as an era when at last the means lie at hand to free mankind from the ancient shackles of pain and of hunger. It is all these things—but I believe the true crisis of our time lies at a deeper level. We have indeed conquered means and resources unknown at earlier ages. We have had thrown open to us frontiers of choice which would have left earlier ages stupefied by their scale and their scope.

But all this freedom and elbow room only thrusts onto us with more force the fundamental issue of the truth that is within us. We can use our wealth, our capacity for some vision of truth, some ideal of brotherhood, or we can imprison ourselves within the selfishness of our own concerns and the limitations of a narrow nationhood. This is the dimension of our crisis.

You may argue that these qualities of dedication, of selflessness, are pretty remote from the realities of politics. They are all very well for private life, but what part can they play in the rough and tumble of partisanship, of primaries, conventions and election campaigns? Ambition, drive, material interests, political skills, the arts of maneuver—all these, you say, have their part, but do not let us pretend that the democratic process is primarily a school of virtue or an arena of moral combat.

And yet, I wonder. It has been the view of great philosphers and great statesmen that our system of free government depends in the first instance upon the virtue of its citizens. Montesquieu made virtue the condition of republican government; Washington declared that it could not survive without it. We have had a hundred and seventy-five years of

it and no one can deny that the system has survived a remarkable amount of skulduggery. In fact, it is probably a
tougher system than its founders imagined. Yet I believe they
are right. For no democratic system can survive without at
least a large and an active leaven of citizens in whom dedication and selflessness are not confined to private life but are
the fundamental principles of their activity in the public
sphere.

Naked interest and ambition will carry a lot of people
naturally and inevitably into politics. We do not need soci-
eties for the promotion of lobbies. Interests, good and bad,
will promote themselves. Nor, in any generation do we lack
politicians whose only principle of action is the advancement
of their own career—the starry-eyed opportunists and all the
other eager men in a hurry to the top. But into what state
must politics degenerate if that is all we find active in the
political arena? That and sectional interests played upon by
personal ambitions? There have been such periods, but our
democratic system survived them because such epochs were
followed and cleansed by periods of disinterested reform.

But there has never been any disinterested reform without disinterested reformers. And here we come to the essential
contribution made by dedication and selflessness to the public
good. No one ever did any good in politics without readiness
for endless hard work—for the grinding, boring, tedious work,
as well as the glamorous, high-sounding, headline-hitting
work. The painstaking hours collecting the facts, the hours
in committee and conference, the hours in persuasion and
argument, the hours of defeat and disappointment, the hours
of disgust and revulsion at the darker sides of human behavior—these cannot be supported without energy and devotion. No reform comes easy; even the most obvious will
have its entrenched enemies. Each one is carried to us on the
bent and the weary backs of patient, dedicated men and
women.

They are not only dedicated in their readiness to give

energy and work to the cause; they must also have sufficiently clear sight and open minds and hearts to see the need for reform in the first place. But clear sight or an open heart for the needs of others is again something that hardly "comes naturally." We have so many needs of our own—our families, our jobs, our homes, our fortunes, our prospects. We are hemmed in with needs and interests, weighty, urgent, honorable, human needs and interests, even if they are exclusively our own. It takes an extra dimension of vision to see beyond our inner circle of personal interest. Most people, most of the time, do not possess it, that extra dimension of vision, which is one reason why self-regarding interests make up so much of the stuff of politics. And this, I suppose, is why the men and women of genuine, imperturbable public spirit seem so few and far between.

I sometimes think there is a danger of this element of vision vanishing almost wholly from our political life. In the main we are so comfortable; so many evils of the past have shrunk in size and almost out of sight. At the same time, people marry much younger; they have larger families and are profoundly involved in earning a living, making careers and safeguarding the future of their children. It is more difficult, they say, to give time to public affairs when private life is so urgent and so absorbing.

Yet is it, I wonder, more urgent and absorbing than it was a hundred years ago, when men not only married young, had large families, built up careers, but also opened up the new frontiers, created new cities out of the wilderness and gave to new states and communities the framework of active political life?

If one reads the story of young Abraham Lincoln, it is hard to believe that his struggles as a young lawyer, his difficulties as a young parent were less than those of young men today. Yet there was no time when the deepest issues of the day did not occupy his mind or the call of statecraft make itself heard above the claims and clamor of everyday life. Nor was he alone or exceptional. Stephen Douglas' life was no different. The prairie towns were filled with earnest, active citizens deeply, profoundly concerned with the great issues of a nation "half slave, half free." When the multitudes gathered, a hundred years ago, to listen in rapt attention for hours to the Lincoln-Douglas debates, had they fewer responsibilities and duties than the citizens of today to many of whom the great issues of politics seem to be most usefully conveyed in a fifteen-second television flash of subliminal advertising?

Is it not possible that the pressures of personal responsibilities are not greater but that the dedication and selflessness needed to discern and to influence public issues have shrunk? In a century in which so many of the mentors of the public mind—from the psychiatrists to the ad-men—speak to us in terms of "what we owe ourselves," may there not indeed have been a slackening of devotion compared with those days, not so long distant, when what man owes to God and his neighbor was a common theme of public discourse?

If so, this is a dangerous hour for our politics and for government by consent of the governed. For at no time have so many of the great issues of the day demanded clear, real moral vision to bring them into focus—the vision, if you please, of A. Powell Davies, who loved the truth and believed in man's capacity and right to govern himself.

A NOTE ON THE SOURCES

PRIMARY SOURCES:

Elizabeth Stevenson Ives, *My Brother Adlai,* New York: Morrow, 1955.

Stevenson Papers, Newberry Library, Chicago.

Stevenson Papers, United Nations.

Papers on the 1960 "Draft Stevenson" Movement, Archives of the Syracuse University Library.

Correspondence, 1953-1965, between Adlai E. Stevenson and the author.

BOOKS BY ADLAI E. STEVENSON:

Major Campaign Speeches of 1952, New York: Random House, 1953.

Call to Greatness, New York: Harper and Bros., 1954.

What I think, New York: Harper and Bros., 1956.

The New America, New York: Harper and Bros., 1957.

Friends and Enemies, New York: Harper and Bros., 1959.

Putting First Things First, New York: Random House, 1960.

Looking Outward, New York: Harper and Row, 1963.

SECONDARY SOURCES:

Stuart Gerry Brown, *Conscience in Politics: Adlai E. Stevenson in the 1950's,* Syracuse: Syracuse University Press, 1961.

Irving S. Davis, *Prophet in His Own Country: The Triumphs and Defeats of Adlai E. Stevenson,* New York: Doubleday, 1957.

216